The
Professional
Edge

The
Professional
Edge

Competencies
in Public Service

James S. Bowman, Jonathan P. West,
Evan M. Berman, and Montgomery Van Wart

M.E.Sharpe
Armonk, New York
London, England

Library of Congress Cataloging-in-Publication Data

The professional edge : competencies in public service / by James S.
Bowman ... [et al.].
   p. cm.
   ISBN 0-7656-1145-7 (cloth : alk. paper) — ISBN 0-7656-1146-5 (pbk.: alk. paper)
   1. Public administration. 2. Civil service positions. 3. Public officers. 4. Nonprofit
organizations—Employees. 5. Executives. 6. Human services personnel. 7. Service
industries workers. 8. Professional employees. 9. Vocational qualifications. I. Bowman,
James S., 1945-

JF1351 .P75 2004
352.3—dc22   2003023977

Printed in the United States of America

The paper used in this publication meets the minimum requirements of
American National Standard for Information Sciences
Permanence of Paper for Printed Library Materials,
ANSI Z 39.48-1984.

∞

BM (c)	10	9	8	7	6	5	4	3	2	1
BM (p)	10	9	8	7	6	5	4	3	2	1

Dedication

For Loretta and all those who value professional ideals—*JSB*
For Colleen M. West and Allan M. West,
consummate public servants—*JPW*
For Dira—*EMB*
For Paul—*MVW*

Contents

List of Tables, Figures, and Exhibits

Tables

Figures

Exhibits

Preface

The new context and character of public service—shifting values, eroding human capital, surging entrepreneurship, exploding information technology, developing performance management, emerging multisector careers, spreading contracting reforms, a diminishing managerial corps, shocking internal economic and external security threats—requires enhanced professional technical, ethical, and leadership competencies. Indeed, each of these competencies is needed in all three arenas of public service: government agencies, nonprofit organizations, and private vendors. Professionalism emphasizes both technical skills (to do "things right") and ethical skills (to do "right things"). Together, they are key to defining leadership. The resulting responsibility—the professional edge—is clear: It is simply unthinkable not to do one's best to improve the quality of democracy.

This book examines components of public service professionalism—excellence in technique, ethics, and leadership for the new century. The possession of only some, but not all, of these elements is insufficient. The business, nonprofit, and governmental debacles of the ongoing Enron Era, for instance, reveal that talented professionals in each sector sacrificed the independent judgment they claimed to possess. In contrast, authentic professionals integrate the technocratic, ethical, and leadership dimensions of their craft as dramatically demonstrated by the 9/11/01 emergency teams. Public service today must be led by consummate professionals steeped in both technical and ethical competencies. The pursuit of quality—made all the more difficult, but more necessary, in turbulent times—requires the robust practice of public service.

Chapter 1, "Public Service Today: Complex, Contradictory, Competitive," briefly reviews the transition from the "old" public service (government-centered functions characterized by lifelong careers and cumbersome bureaucracy) to the "new" public service (multisectored activities featuring short-term jobs and dynamic network-like structures). How postmodern trends create a heightened need for professional proficiencies is then explored.

The next three chapters scrutinize what it means to be a true public servant—that is, someone with subject matter background and moral imagination who is prepared to lead. Chapter 2, "The Technical Professional: Developing Expertise," probes the faculties needed and links these with performance management, human resource administration, and information technology skills. Chapter 3, "The Ethical Professional: Cultivating Scruples," investigates values, professional moral development, decision-making tools, and organizational integrity. Chapter 4, "The Consummate Professional: Creating Leadership," focuses on assessment and goal setting, personal characteristics and behaviors, evaluation, and how specialized knowledge and ethical bearing are integral to true professionalism. Realistic contemporary scenarios and personal skill-building exercises appear in each of these chapters.

Finally, Chapter 5, "The Future of Public Service: Cases and Commentary for the New Millennium," explores professional challenges in the years ahead. Both mundane and dramatic cases illustrate how government, business, and nonprofit officials—as managers of the state—must master professional competencies.

The classic definition—and vow—of a professional is leadership in technical competency and ethical character. "Our lives," Martin Luther King once observed, "begin to end the day that we become silent about things that matter." The ability to contemplate, enhance, and act upon these three faculties is the essence of professional life. Those dedicated to excellence, and who use the text to cultivate their capacity for critical judgment—the *sine qua non* of a professional—will get the most out of this book.

Acknowledgments

The authors are pleased to acknowledge Steve Condrey, Carole Jurkiewicz, Barbara Apostolou, Dennis Wittmer, Paul Suino, Howard Rassmussen, Nathalia Gillot, and Emily Joseph who read all, or parts of, drafts of this book. Any remaining errors are the responsibility of the authors.

The
Professional
Edge

— Chapter 1 —

Public Service Today
Complex, Contradictory, Competitive

*There is no higher religion than human service. To
work for the common good is the greatest creed.*
—Woodrow Wilson

*Joshua Bennett was excited to start work as a management ana-
lyst in his southeastern state's human resource department immediately upon graduation with his Masters of Public Administration
degree. During his six-month probationary period, he was given
varied assignments of increasing difficulty. While he had to struggle
with some of these, he gained confidence at the end of his probation and his performance evaluation was satisfactory. Joshua is
now ending his first full year of employment. He likes his job, but
he is concerned that he lacks the skills to successfully complete
the complex assignments he is now receiving as the state adapts to
electronic government. At the time of his hiring he was promised
job-related training and resources to equip him with the necessary
information technology skills to meet performance expectations.
Such hardware, software, and technical training has not been provided. Job stress and frustration result from his inability to satis-
factorily complete recent assignments.*

    *Maria Rodriguez has worked for twenty years as a clinical psy-
chologist in a nonprofit hospital on the West Coast. She derives
substantial satisfaction from her work and feels that she is making
a difference in the lives of her patients. Her accomplishments have
been recognized with awards, promotions, and certificates of appreciation. Two years ago the chief of staff appointed her to the
hospital's ethics committee and last month she was made chair of
the committee. The thorny problems brought to this committee,*

3

often involving new medical technologies and changing mana-
gerial philosophies or fiscal policies, have occupied an increas-
ing amount of Maria's time and attention. The most recent issue
has her perplexed. The case involves a conflict between protect-
ing the privacy of patient records and meeting the reimburse-
ment requirements of third-party payers. Maria is concerned that
the hospital's administrative and fiscal requirements are com-
promising patient care, with specific ethical implications for par-
ticular patients and legal issues for the hospital. Maria is
uncertain how to proceed.

Regina Blackstone is a research specialist in a large corpora-
tion located in a midwestern state. She has training as a researcher
and over the years has produced several reports that have contrib-
uted to her growing reputation as a knowledgeable expert on tech-
nical issues. As a staff person she has operated mainly in a support
or advisory role, often in relative isolation from others. Recently
the firm bid for and received a government contract to deliver a
city service. Regina's boss asked her to lead this effort. She quickly
accepted the position, feeling flattered to be tapped for this re-
sponsibility. A few weeks later, however, Regina is apprehensive
about her ability to spearhead this new initiative. She fears that
she may personify the "Peter Principle," having been promoted to
her highest level of competence previously, but now she's been
advanced to a level at which she will be incompetent. Her aca-
demic preparation as a data analyst, her corporate background as
a researcher, and her lack of public sector experience provided
few opportunities to master the new leadership skills required. She
is reluctant to relinquish her new job, but is nervous and unsure
about what to do next.

Joshua, Maria, and Regina are dedicated professionals, each with
a unique challenge that affects performance. These challenges in
part are a result of a shift from the old public service to the new
public service that requires a different set of professional competencies. Joshua works for state government, Maria does public
service in the nonprofit arena, and Regina's new assignment with

her private contracting firm will require bridge building with the public sector. All three are feeling poorly prepared for their current assignments: Joshua lacks the technical skills required to complete routine tasks necessitated by recent developments in information technology; Maria needs help resolving dilemmas linked to changes in the legal and ethical environment; and Regina has a skills deficit that may compromise her ability to lead a private-public partnership.

The situations confronting these three individuals illustrate the thesis of this chapter: The dynamic external and internal environment creates the need for professional managers who possess technical, ethical, and leadership competencies to meet the complex governance challenges of the twenty-first century. This chapter begins with a brief summary of the changing context of public service. It then contrasts the characteristics of the old and new citizen service, and clarifies the meaning of contemporary public service. Finally, it analyzes the three dimensions of professionalism —technical, ethical, and leadership skills—that result in the "professional edge." Here the focus is on why these skills are so important in today's turbulent environment. Subsequent chapters show how such competencies may be acquired.

Changing Context

The rapidly changing external environment—corporate globalism, cybertechnology, changing values and management philosophies— has greatly affected the delivery of public services. The explosion of information technologies alone, as Joshua and Maria's experience illustrates, raises new technical and ethical issues, unknown as recently as a few years ago, and requires new skills. Similarly, supranational organizations, such as the World Trade Organization, world environmental groups, multinational corporations, and other nongovernmental organizations, help shape American policy and its implementation by public servants. Likewise, changes in the internal environment of public service—increased sector mobility, privatization, and devolution—require rethinking of who provides services and how they are delivered. Regina's task of directing her firm's contracting effort to provide a public service, for example, is one facing managers in many private and nonprofit organizations both in the United States and abroad.

Clearly the workplace of today's public service professional is in constant flux, causing apprehension and uncertainty, but also providing opportunities and challenges. Leicht and Fennell (2001) identify six key characteristics of today's workplace: (a) flatter organizational hierarchies, (b) more temporary workers, (c) wide use of subcontracting and outsourcing, (d) massive downsizing of permanent workers, (e) a post-union bargaining environment, and (f) virtual organizations. The public servant—whether working for government, nonprofits, or business firms—understands that these changes affect the way they work. The emergence of virtual and flatter organizations is made easier as employers like Joshua's move to e-government. Regina's new responsibilities in supervising and overseeing her firm's delivery of service are indicative of the movement to both subcontract, and, eventually, in many places, downsize permanent employees and increase temporary government workers. These moves are easier to accomplish in a more flexible, post-union bargaining environment.

Changing Nature of Public Service: From Old to New

Significant changes are also occurring in the way public service is conceived. Relevant research in the past (e.g., Mosher 1982), and to a lesser extent today (e.g., Volcker 2003), emphasizes government-centered work. More recently, however, the blurring of the boundaries between government, private, and nonprofit sectors has given public service a broader meaning. The changing profile of the profession has meant that public service no longer refers exclusively to tasks performed by government; it now involves work with not-for-profit organizations and private firms as well. Thus, multisectored service providers, mobility or sector switching among employers, and commitment of individuals to make a difference animate the tectonic shift occurring in public service (Light 1999: 127–28).

Building on this characterization (see also Mosher 1982; Sherwood 2000), public service is "the people establishment" that delivers services to citizens, promotes the collective interest, and accepts the resulting obligations. Individuals, representing different sectors of the economy, who provide a wide array of services, advance the general welfare, and uphold the public trust are part of the public service. They may work in city, county, state, or federal government; for a nonprofit hospital, school, or charitable organization; or for a business contractor.

Indeed, the contemporary public service professional is as likely as not to be a salaried employee of an organization in one of these sectors as government, public, not-for-profit, private bureaucracies have become professionalized. Professionalism is defined by the need for specialized knowledge whose application is critical to address complex problems of social welfare (Exhibit 1.1).

The craft of public service, like the practice of medicine, is much more than knowing specialized skills; rather, the consummate professional is defined by the responsible exercise of discretion. This demands judgments by leaders that are both technically and morally sound. Public service magnifies these considerations in two ways. First, many problems are not "tame" or technical ones that have straightforward solutions (e.g., how to build a highway); rather they are "wicked" or political ones that have only imperfect, temporary solutions (e.g., where to build a highway). The challenge is that officials must attempt to "correct" wicked problems in order to make them manageable. Second, whatever decisions are made come to be seen as "moral and absolute," as they publicly represent both the symbolic and real authoritative allocation of values in a society. Whether the service is delivered by a government, nonprofit, or private organization it remains a public responsibility. It is exactly the public acceptance of responsibility that provides professionals with an "edge" that distinguishes them from others and thereby furnishes the "right stuff." This is the key to the identity and legitimacy of public service.

The consummate professional, then, reflects a triangle of complementary competencies—technical expertise (the "how"), ethical

Exhibit 1.1

Models of Professionalism

While definitional controversies and occupational comparisons have a very long history, two models—trait-based and decision-based—clarify the nature of professionalism. The first focuses on a set of commonly used ideal criteria to characterize a profession:

- a specialized competence,
- autonomy in exercising this competence,
- commitment to a career in the competence,
- a service orientation,
- a professional association, and
- a code of conduct to encourage the proper use of competence.

In contrast, the second model emphasizes the actual working of a profession: the significance of the tasks it confronts, the esoteric nature of the decision-making process, and the capacity to resolve problems. That is, the layperson seeks help precisely because the problem is critical, the analytical process is technical and opaque, and a solution is possible. Each of these frameworks implies the classic definition—and vow—of a professional leader: excellence in technical competence and moral character (Bowman 1998). The characteristics and competencies embodied in such models indicate how a profession may distinguish itself from other occupations.

Traditionally there were just three recognized professions, law, medicine, and religion, but the concept in contemporary times encompasses a wide variety of pursuits. Although some endeavors are arguably "more professional" than others (envision a continuum from the least to the most professionalized), individual practitioners can be recognized as professionals because of their skills and behaviors regardless of whether their occupation as a whole possesses each of the attributes in the above models. If a majority of practitioners conduct themselves in a professional manner, then the field is a profession. Professional status is a worthy objective for those charged with protection of the public trust. The new public service, in fact, may be seen as an "umbrella" profession, insofar as public service employs highly trained people from all sectors of the economy.

integrity (the "why"), and leadership (the "what") in his/her field. Conscious that one's activities have significance beyond the immediate situation, the professional avoids a simple "bottom-line" mentality; rather than society serving the economy, it is the economy that serves society. The standard is not *caveat emptor* ("let the buyer beware"), but *credat emptor* ("let the buyer trust"). Software programmers are concerned about writing "cool" code, teachers about educating students, program analysts about doing thorough studies, and health care providers about helping patients. Success is gauged by how decisions define the history and future of the profession in society. When such ideals are realized, the points of the triangle are in harmony and the compromise of excellence unlikely.

While the locus and composition of public service have changed, the primary purpose continues to be the improvement of civic well-being. This improvement may take many forms, as Robert and Janet Denhardt (2001: 19) have said of public servants, "Service to the public—helping people in trouble, making the world safer and cleaner, helping children to learn and prosper, literally going where others would not go—is our job and our calling." They observe that "This ability to be selfless, to be open to the needs and values and wants of others, is a part of each public servant" (Denhardt and Denhardt 2001: 19). Specific examples are heroic, selfless emergency workers in the aftermath of the 9/11 attacks. Less dramatic, but critically important, is the work of safety inspectors, educators, scientists, researchers, intelligence gatherers, social workers, regulators, dam builders, court personnel, transportation employees, corrections officers, social service providers, and numerous others.

This list is not exhaustive, but is merely a sampling of public service. It is hard to define, but easy to recognize, much like U.S. Supreme Court Justice Potter Stewart's famous response when asked to clarify the meaning of obscenity: "I know it when I see it." As with the Oldsmobile of another era, "your father's public service" is not that of this generation. The following two sections briefly look backward and then forward by comparing key differences between the old and the new public service.

The Old Public Service

The defining characteristics of the old public service are a product of industrial era government—those who comprised the old public service were government workers carrying out functions in centralized, hierarchical bureaucracies according to routine standard operating procedures. Their discretion was limited by their position in the vertical chain of command and they were accountable to their superiors. Elected officials set public policy, defined the public interest, and monitored program management. Authority flowed from top to bottom, services were provided directly to citizens, control or regulation was government centered, staff roles were clear, and skills were specialized. Civil service protection was granted to permanent employees whose pay and benefits came directly from government.

While President Bill Clinton proclaimed in the mid-1990s that "the era of big government is over," it depends on how data are interpreted. The public workforce in 1999 was in excess of 20 million, up from both 1990 (18.4 million) and 1980 (16.2 million), with most of those workers and most of the growth occurring in local and state jurisdictions. Indeed, the era of big *federal* government growth appears to be over at present, and the size of the federal workforce has actually declined in recent years. However, despite downsizing, right sizing, privatizing, and outsourcing, the size of the public sector workforce has not shrunk, especially at state and local levels. The pre–9/11 mantra, "the era of big government is over," is over. And, privatization, contracting, and public-private partnering have increased. Public service contracting is most often used in services such as waste collection, building maintenance, bill collecting, data processing, health and medical, and street cleaning and repair (Andrisani, Hakim, and Leeds 2000). Nonprofit corporations' share of total paid employment in the United States was 9.3 percent in 1998, up from 7.3 percent in 1977 (Jalandoni et al. 2002), and many government contracts for such services are negotiated with nonprofit organizations. The rest are with the private sector.

The move to cut back and outsource services is seen as an opportunity by some and a threat by others. It is an opportunity to those who wish to see government operate more like a business that is cost and quality conscious. It is a threat to those employed by government and the unions representing them who fear job loss and service deterioration. Because government workers are much more likely to be unionized than their private sector counterparts (38 percent vs. 9 percent), labor opposition to restructuring along corporate lines is not surprising. The post-union bargaining environment noted by Leicht and Fennell (2001) is clearly more descriptive of the private sector workplace than the public sector.

While government-run public service continues to directly provide some goods and services by civil servants, and will do so for the foreseeable future, this is changing rapidly. U.S. Comptroller General David Walker believes that "The government is on a 'burning platform' and the status-quo way of doing business is unacceptable" (quoted in Keene 2003: 15). This perception that the old ways are no longer up to the new tasks has prompted new actors using new instruments of civic action to emerge to meet citizen needs. This necessitates a rethinking of government's role, composition, and management agenda (see Exhibits 1.2 and 1.3) as well as a more realistic definition of the new public service. The future portends a smaller role for government, an enlarged nonprofit sector, and an increase in public-private partnerships or contractual relationships with business.

The New Public Service

The new public service has a different set of defining characteristics more suitable to a post-industrial, service-based economy (see Denhardt and Denhardt 2003). Today vertical hierarchy is giving way to horizontal "networks," bureaucracies are diminishing, and shared leadership structures are emerging. The public interest is identified and pursued as a collaborative process based on dialogue with relevant stakeholders. The discretion of empowered administrative officials is present, but limited, and they remain accountable to the citizens via elected political leaders and administrative oversight. Employee job boundaries are flexible and skill sets are versatile.

Exhibit 1.2

A New Management Agenda for the Federal Government?

In the short term the outbreak of terrorism in the United States has prompted the president to establish an Office of Homeland Security [now Department of Homeland Security], partial federalization of airport security, legislation broadening the powers of law enforcement agencies, substantial extraordinary appropriations and related measures. . . . (I)n the longer term terrorism may serve as the catalyst for a new agenda for a new period of public administration. . . . This formative agenda goes beyond conventional contemporary concerns with efficiency and performance measurement, and the current belief that downsizing government, devolving federal responsibilities and marketizing public action will solve public problems.

This new agenda will be shaped by answers to the three questions that have defined previous periods. . . .

- What are the purposes, missions and roles of the federal government in American and world society?
- What values should the federal government respect, protect, and promote?
- What organizational forms, human and technical investments, and methods and technologies should the federal government employ in pursuing these purposes, missions, roles, and values?

Today only tentative and speculative answers are possible. . . . The shift towards strategic, longer term thinking will accelerate. The reason is threefold: (1) the demographic imperatives of the entitlement state—which now commands 60 percent to 70 percent of federal expenditures or well over a trillion dollars a year . . . (2) . . . terrorism poses profound and important long-term challenges to the nation and to governance . . . (3) a unifying, long range, comprehensive framework of federal missions and roles is required for identifying and making scientific and technological investments and choices. . . .

(continued)

Exhibit 1.2 *(continued)*

The Government Performance and Results Act (GPRA) of 1993 has been construed to require strategic planning and measurement directed to agency policy missions and program results—but not to the achievement of democratic and constitutional values. These non-mission values—due process of law, fairness in contract competition and public representation—are excluded from strategic planning and measurement. . . . This premise reflects the notion prevalent in the 1990s that government is a business and should be managed as such. In the emerging era management for results under the GPRA almost certainly will be extended to include management that takes into account democratic and constitutional results and values. . . .

At its core, the failure of the federal government to develop an institutional capacity to plan for long-run trends. . . . arises from the fragmentation and dispersion of power over federal management in the presidency, Congress, agencies and political networks . . . Can greater coherence be achieved? . . . Conventional wisdom says no, but conventional wisdom may be wrong. . . . In every major period of the nation's history, in response to crises and perceived national needs, members of Congress, presidents and public activists have forged coalitions to restructure, redefine and redirect public power and federal management to achieve national goals. . . . The question is whether this generation will contribute . . . and how, so that the long-range problems and opportunities confronting the nation can be effectively addressed.

Source: Carroll (2002: 9). Copyright © 2002 American Society for Public Administration. Reprinted with permission.

The transition from the old to the new style of providing services has altered the role of the public sector, "emphasizing collaboration and enablement rather than hierarchy and control" (Salamon 2002: vii).

The new system has been referred to variously as "the new governance," "third-party government," "government by proxy," and "indirect government." While fewer of those managing direct pub-

Exhibit 1.3

Changing Composition of the Old Public Service

Impending retirements and restless workers portend drastic changes in the federal government workforce. It is estimated that over 70 percent of federal workers are eligible to retire between now and 2011 and that a similar percentage of Senior Executive Service members will reach retirement age in 2005. While the U.S. Office of Personnel Management doubts that actual requirements will reach these proportions, such projections raise concerns about loss of institutional memory and lack of knowledge about how to get things done. Some agencies will be especially hard hit: 22 percent of the State Department's civil service employees will have turned sixty in the next five years and another 20 percent will reach age sixty ten years from now. Other departments are taking steps to retain the knowledge of senior employees. For example, the Forest Service is calling back selected retired employees as mentors and both the Department of Veterans Affairs and NASA are using videotapes of senior employees and managers to share the lessons they learned in public service with newcomers. Notwithstanding these initiatives, surveys of senior executives conducted in 2000 reveal that their agencies lacked any formal succession-planning program to replace seasoned senior executives.

A more recent government-wide survey conducted by the U.S. Office of Personnel Management found that over one-third of the 100,000 federal workers surveyed say they are considering leaving their jobs. Slightly fewer than half of the 34.6 percent contemplating departure indicate they plan to retire within three years. While it is unclear whether these workers would seek federal employment elsewhere or whether they plan to leave federal service altogether, findings suggest employees are not "connected" with their jobs. Pay, benefits, and job significance are not the main problem; indeed, satisfaction levels are reasonably high: 68 percent are satisfied with their jobs, 64 percent are satisfied with their pay and their retirement benefits, and nine out of ten feel their

(continued)

Exhibit 1.3 *(continued)*

work is important. What is lacking? Intangible incentives to motivate superior performance: Less than half of those surveyed indicate satisfaction with recognition for a job well done, less than a third believe award programs provide meaningful incentives, 27 percent think management deals effectively with poor performers, and 36 percent indicate leaders spur high motivation among employees.

Federal government managers face the challenge of replacing retiring workers and retaining as well as motivating existing employees.

Source: Adapted from Davidson (2002); C. Lee (2003). Reprinted with permission from ATPCO and the Washington Post, respectively.

lic services are government employees, George Frederickson (2003: 11) observes that those who act for the state are "clothed with the public interest" and "covered with a public purpose." The managerial challenges in light of these changes are substantial, but they are both similar and different from those of prior periods. They are the same in the sense that many of the dominant values from earlier eras—efficiency, economy, fairness, and performance—continue to be important together with renewed emphasis on values associated with citizenship, public interest, ethics, transparency, and broad democratic values of accountability, equity, and responsiveness. The challenges are different in that the production and delivery of goods and services increasingly involves two streams: (a) government as a direct provider and (b) delivery by others acting "indirectly" on government's behalf. Public officials have experience with direct delivery, but must quickly adapt to the demands of indirect government (Kettl 2002a, 2002b).

The transition from command-and-control decision making based on hierarchical authority structures to indirect, web-like relationships in the new era requires, according to Kettl (2002a), a new set of managerial skills: using carrot-and-stick incentives, forging public-private partnerships, making smart purchases, do-ing performance measurement, tracking money, writing contracts, auditing finances and performance, and overseeing service pro-viders. He singles out five skills, in particular, for special attention when managing indirect programs: goal setting, negotiation, com-munication, financial management, and bridge building. New tools, as well, will become more commonplace with the "fuzzy bound-aries" of indirect government, including contracting, grants, vouch-ers, tax expenditures, loan guarantees, and government-sponsored enterprises (Salamon 2002). These and other skills and tools will be considered in greater detail in subsequent sections in this book, but it is important here to stress that a new skill set or toolbox is required of today's public servant who will operate in an environ-ment where indirect government is becoming the norm.

The gradual transition from the old to the new public service alters the role of government, but politics and professionalism have been and will continue to be focal concerns of both the old and the new public service. This subject is the focus of the next section.

Public Service—Politics and Professionalism

American democratic traditions reflect a tension between politi-cal and professional control of the public service. This tension was especially evident in the old (government run) public service, but it is present in the new "networked" public service as well. It plays out differently at various points in the nation's history. In the first four decades following Washington's inauguration, appointed officials in government were drawn from the gentlemanly, aristo-cratic ranks and "fitness" for public service was a key criterion for making appointments. Well-educated, wealthy, white, male land-owners—in short, the privileged elites—were thought to be best suited to positions of high government office. The Jacksonian revo-lution gave greater weight to partisan politics when deciding whom to hire. Jackson helped democratize public service and diminish elitism by hiring those from diverse class and geographic back-grounds. Such appointments were consistent with Jackson's view that government work was so simple that virtually anyone could do it. Implementing his "rotation in office" principle broke the hold of aristocratic entitlement to government offices. During the mid- to late–nineteenth century this rotation meant that the practice "to the victor go the spoils" was followed. With each election, many civil servants were hired based primarily on party affiliation.

Passage of the Pendleton Act in 1883 attempted to depoliticize public service by instituting a merit system at the federal level. Parallel policy initiatives in many states and localities introduced civil service reforms thereafter. Gradually, over the next several decades, "what you knew" (merit) replaced "who you knew" (partisanship) as the key consideration in personnel selection as merit systems became more established. Renewed emphasis was given to rationality, expertise, and professionalism. Today civil service systems, ideally based on merit principles (see Exhibit 1.4), are found at all levels of government; however, they too have become the subject of harsh criticism because they may fall short of the principles they espouse (Pfiffner and Brook 2000). Indeed, states like Georgia and Florida have recently radically reformed their civil service systems reinstituting spoils-like "at-will" employment (Condrey and Maranto 2001; West 2002; Bowman 2002). Furthermore, in most jurisdictions, even those purportedly based on merit, politics has not been removed entirely from the selection process. In many, personal connections and prior service as well as partisan considerations and competence are factored together in making staffing decisions. Appointing officials often seek a blend of loyalty and ability in their new hires.

Historically, the public, too, has been ambivalent about politics versus professionalism as a controlling influence over government appointments. Professionals are admired for their training, expertise, and autonomy, but they are held in lower esteem if they work for government. Political appointees connect government to the rest of society in ways that professional bureaucrats do not, as noted by Dionne, who stresses "citizen service is essential to the health of civil society" (2001: 9). However, those citizen servants appointed to political positions as well as the "bureaucrats" in the

Exhibit 1.4

Federal Merit System Principles

1. Recruit qualified individuals from all segments of society and select and advance employees on the basis of merit after fair and open competition that assures that all receive equal opportunity.
2. Treat employees and applicants fairly and equitably, without regard to political affiliation, race, color, religion, national origin, sex, marital status, age, or handicapping condition, and with proper regard for their privacy and constitutional rights.
3. Provide equal pay for equal work and recognize excellent performance.
4. Maintain high standards of integrity, conduct, and concern for the public interest.
5. Manage employees efficiently and effectively.
6. Retain and separate employees on the basis of their performance.
7. Educate and train employees when it will result in better organizational or individual performance.
8. Protect employees from arbitrary action, personal favoritism, or coercion for partisan political purposes.
9. Protect employees against reprisal for the lawful disclosure of information in "whistleblower" situations (i.e., protecting people who report things like illegal and/or wasteful activities).

Source: U.S. Department of the Interior, www.doi.gov/hrm/pmanager/gm2d.html.

civil service are too often described as either "hacks" or "bumblers." Despite such an overdrawn characterization, in part reinforced by scandal-seeking media and "bureaucrat-bashing" politicians, the clear trend has been for increased professionalism in the public sector workforce. Government employs a disproportionately large number of white-collar workers who fall into the professional, technical, and administrative U.S. Census categories. This increased professionalism is necessary due to the growing complexity of the work to be done. Andrew Jackson's view of government work as "simple" has not been accurate for many generations.

The American political system continues to rely heavily on politically.appointed "citizen servants," who, while amateurs, bring fresh ideas and reinvigorate governmental operations when a newly elected chief executive enters office. A powerful, professional ruling class has not emerged in the United States as it has in other countries. Furthermore, in an era where privatization, partnerships, and outsourcing are increasingly common, we count on both "citizen service" and professional civil service to oversee the "network" of those who directly deliver public services; indeed, many of these service providers are professionals themselves. Nonetheless, "cozy politics" sometimes surrounds decisions to privatize or contract for public services (Kobrak 2002), challenging professional values and norms of operation.

Paradoxically, flat organizational structures, decentralized service delivery, employee empowerment, and virtual organizations simultaneously provide both opportunities and threats for professional public servants. The independence, autonomy, and expertise associated with professionalism are given freer rein under the more flexible arrangements found in the new public service. At the same time the loss of traditional controls provides opportunities for corner cutting, self-interested behaviors, uneven or inequitable service delivery, and conflicts of interest. Government oversight continues to be crucial to curbing these excesses as evidenced by massive accounting fraud at flagship corporations (e.g., Enron, Global Crossing, WorldCom, Tyco), investment banks, and mutual funds (see Exhibit 1.5 and chapter 5). The challenge of today's public servant, whether located inside or outside of government, is to be politically adept by being attuned to the conflicting currents that must be navigated. She must also be professionally astute by having the requisite technical, ethical, and leadership skills to both do the right things and do things right. This challenge will be the focus of the next section.

Exhibit 1.5

In Oversight We Trust

We have the same excesses as other capitalist nations have, because fear and greed are built into capitalism. What distinguishes America is our system's ability to consistently expose, punish, regulate and ultimately reform those excesses—better than any other [country]. How often do you hear about such problems being exposed in Mexico or Argentina, Russia or China? They may have all the hardware of capitalism, but they don't have all the software—namely, an uncorrupted bureaucracy to manage the regulatory agencies, licensing offices, property laws and commercial courts.

Indeed, what foreigners envy us most for is precisely the city that some love to bash: Washington. That is, they envy us for our alphabet soup of regulatory agencies: the SEC, the Federal Reserve, the FAA, the FDA, the FBI, the EPA, the IRS, and INS. Do you know what a luxury it is to be able to start a business or get a license without having to pay off some official? Sure, we have our bad apples, but most of our bureaucrats are pretty decent. In fact, our federal bureaucrats are to capitalism what the New York Police and Fire Departments were to 9/11—the unsung guardians of America's civic religion, the religion that says if you work hard and play by the rules, you'll get rewarded and you won't get ripped off.

Well, count me among those naïve fools with a fundamental belief in the federal government—not because I have no faith in ordinary Americans, but because I have no trust in ordinary Big Oil, ordinary Enron or ordinary Harken Energy to do the right thing without proper oversight. . . . What triggered the 489-point one-day rise in the Dow? It was word that Congress had agreed on a plan to create a new independent oversight board for the accounting industry. Much of America's moral authority to lead the world derives from the decency of our government and its bureaucrats, and the example we set for others. These are not things to be sneered at. They are things to be cherished, strengthened and praised every single day.

Source: Excerpted from Friedman (2002: 13). Copyright © 2002 The New York Times Co. Reprinted with permission.

Figure 1.1 **The Skills Triangle of Public Service Professionalism**

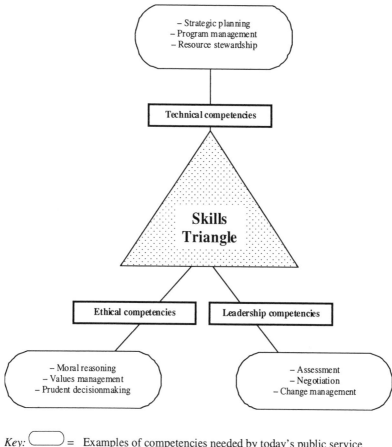

Key: ⬭ = Examples of competencies needed by today's public service professionals.

The Skills Triangle

Figure 1.1 depicts the Skills Triangle that provides an analytical framework for the remainder of this chapter and those to follow. Today's public service requires skills in three key areas: technical, ethical, and leadership competencies. Their mastery is essential for the consummate professional.

Technical Competencies

Competence in one's chosen field is a hallmark of professionalism. Entailing many functional specialties (e.g., budgeting) and substantive fields (e.g., health care), public service technical skills include strategic planning, program management, and resource stewardship (Exhibit 1.6). Citizens reasonably expect competent performance from all public servants, especially in a post–9/11 environment (see Exhibit 1.6), and when incompetence is uncovered the legitimacy of the public service suffers. Mastery of basic planning functions, effective program management, and resource stewardship is essential in today's results-oriented environment.

To briefly illustrate the importance of technical proficiency four skills are isolated: (a) job task mastery, (b) project management, (c) information technology, and (d) productivity improvement. Given the vast array of public services provided, these areas are deliberately broad and involve skills that cut across sectors, organizations, and roles. Citizens, elected public officials, boards of directors, and stockholders evaluate professionals in the new public service, in part, based on their competencies in these areas.

First, job task mastery is expected of any manager or employee regardless of their position or employer. In the scenario opening this chapter, Joshua Bennett had mastered the requisite skills during his probation period, but several months later he felt ill equipped to meet his growing responsibilities. Virtual technology applications in Joshua's field now involve use of software for many tasks, including payroll and benefits, job analysis and job descriptions, performance appraisal, and position classification (West and Berman 2001). Web-based training, computer-based personnel testing, training management software as well as computerized interviews and background checks are used in many governmental, private, and nonprofit organizations. Without proper training, public servants will be unprepared for the transition from traditional to virtual human resource management. Responsibility for career planning and development is shifting from employers to employees; skill deficits related to job mastery of the kind Joshua is experiencing ought not go unaddressed.

Exhibit 1.6

Workforce Priority

The tumultuous events of 2001 have prompted everyone, including government, to take stock of priorities. Naturally, the focus of government—and the nation as a whole—is correctly fixed upon the task at hand, which is to thwart and defeat terrorism. But the government must not lose sight of its ongoing challenge of ensuring it has the skilled workforce it will need in the years ahead.

The events of 9/11 and their aftermath demonstrated to the world the remarkable capability and resilience of the United States and its government to respond to severe crises. After the attacks, virtually every department abruptly changed course to direct resources and staff to more pressing needs. They dispensed loans to small businesses injured by the attacks, investigated terrorists and their finances, secured the borders and airports, prepared for biochemical threats, developed plans to protect key infrastructure targets, waged war in Afghanistan, and carried out other tasks.

In many cases, the politically appointed leaders at those departments were not yet in place. Nevertheless, dedicated and experienced career civil servants across the federal government responded quickly and effectively to the many crises spawned on 9/11.

Now, many employees are aging and will soon retire. Replacing these federal employees will not be easy. It is a problem that will not go away. It is a problem that threatens the government's ability to respond to such crises in the future. And, as we witnessed this year, it is a problem that ultimately affects us all.

Source: "Workforce Priority," *Federal Times,* December 31, 2001, 18. Reprinted with permission.

Second, competencies in program and project management are necessary for those in the new public service, and these competencies are now more complicated as informal teamwork and collaboration blur the lines among departments, organizations, sectors, and jurisdictions. A practical framework and management skill set is needed to administer programs so that public servants achieve their objectives in a timely manner. This includes abilities in organization, planning, work definition, scheduling, budgeting, risk management, logistics, technical reviews and audits, and evaluation.

Thus, for example, public servants require familiarity with the project planning process and the tools associated with it. During the planning phase, time and cost estimates are necessary, and at the outset user surveys and needs assessments must be conducted. Implementation requires assigning responsibility for each task with its attendant costs, and tools such as Gannt charts or Program Evaluation and Review Technique (PERT) charts may be used. In addition, motivation and leadership issues need to be addressed. Finally, monitoring and evaluation is necessary (see Berman 1998). Matrix organizations and cross-institutional collaboration on projects complicate project management and challenge the technical skills of those in the new public service.

Third, new information technology (IT) is influencing all aspects of management. In the opening vignettes, Joshua Bennett tries to master the technical IT skills in his job, as Maria Rodriguez copes with ethical issues associated with patient privacy and the use of new medical technologies. Information technologies now enable people to "work together apart" in distant locations, and virtual interactions can occur without all parties being physically present. Use of IT innovations (e.g., e-mail and discussion groups) change the way work is done and increase opportunities for "boundary spanning," an important advantage in the collaborative work of the new public service. Laggards in learning to cope with these new technologies will remain behind unless they quickly gain IT skills.

Finally, pressures to improve productivity are features of both the old and new public service. Quality management, process reengineering, and performance measurement are prominent reforms. Paul Light (1997: ch. 1) has identified four reform tides that have ebbed and flowed over the past several decades and the primary values associated with each: The emphasis on efficiency and economy is correlated with reform tides originating in scientific management and the war on waste, while fairness is linked to the watchful eye tide, and performance improvement is tied to the more recent liberation management tide.

Figure 1.2 **Importance of Productivity Values by Sector**

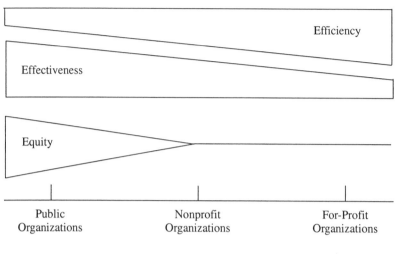

Source: Berman (1998: 9).

Efficiency, equity, and effectiveness are longstanding produc-
tivity-related values emphasized in business, nonprofit, and public administration. With the increase in public-private partnerships
that cut across the three sectors, there will need to be mutual adjustments in the relative emphasis of these fundamental values.
Figure 1.2 depicts the importance of productivity values in each of
the three sectors. As Berman notes:

> Productivity is defined as the effective and efficient use of resources.
> Effectiveness is typically of great importance in the public sector, and
> nonprofit organizations often emphasize effectiveness and efficiency in
> equal measure. Public sector organizations also value providing services
> to all population groups, thereby ensuring equity. (Berman 1998: 9)

Those in the new public service involved in public-private partnerships will need to combine technical mastery of various productivity improvement tools and strategies with an awareness of
the relative importance given to these values in different settings.

Ethical Competencies

The second point of the skills triangle refers to ethical capacity. To cope with the changes in the external and internal environment, public servants need to buttress technical skills with ethical competencies, such as moral reasoning, values management, and prudent decisionmaking. Social scientists and journalists are fond of displaying thermometer charts showing the decline in public trust in government since the 1960s. Indeed, the drop in confidence has been dramatic—from over three-quarters who in the mid-1960s said they trust government in Washington to do the right thing "most of the time" to 29 percent today (Mackenzie and Labiner 2002). While there was an increase in trust immediately following 9/11 (30 percent in 2000 vs. 64 percent in late September 2001), trust levels are now near where they were earlier (Morin and Deane 2002).

Those in the public service can help to rebuild citizen confidence by further demonstrating to the populace that they are worthy of that trust. They can further reinforce confidence by ensuring that those delivering services—inside or outside of government—are in compliance with professional best practices. Adhering to high standards of conduct, minimizing partisanship, avoiding scandals, spending monies wisely, and being responsive to citizens help as well. Perhaps the most important thing they can do is to exercise their discretion wisely by making prudent decisions. In other words, those in the professional public service need to do the right things.

Beyond these general observations what are some specific ethical skills and competencies and why are they needed? Four abilities will be discussed here for purposes of illustration (additional skills and ways to develop them will be considered in chapter 4): (a) principled moral reasoning, (b) recognition of ethics-related conflicts, (c) refusal to do something unethical, and (d) application of ethical theory.

The literature on principled moral reasoning is voluminous, attesting to its importance as a skill to be mastered. Lawrence Kohlberg (1981) holds that people differ in the way they respond to dilemmas and that their thought processes can provide the basis

Table 1.1

A Six-Step Model of Ethical Reasoning

Steps	Questions to be considered
1. Gathering data	What are the facts? What is the ethical issue? What is right or wrong in this situation? Must anything be known before considering a course of action?
2. Developing alternatives	What can be done? What is the moral tension between alternatives? Do options detract from the organization's mission? Do options strengthen relationships with stake-holders? Is each alternative consistent with the decision maker's personal ethics?
3. Forecasting outcomes	What will happen? What would make the situation right? Have all probable outcomes been identified?
4. Applying criteria to the outcomes	What should be done? What ethical principles would justify the action? Are they of equal importance?
5. Selecting an action	How should it be done? What course of action is feasible? How do organizational policies and the law affect the decision?
6. Evaluating behavior	What difference did the action make? Did it have the desired outcome? What follow-up is needed?

Sources: Adapted from Wartick and Wood (1998); Anderson (1996); Aulisio, Arnold, and Youngner (2000).

for categorizing them into one of three levels (each with two stages of moral development; chapter 3). Diagnostic instruments have been developed that can help identify one's stage of moral development. Such knowledge is useful because challenging ethical issues require the mastery of moral reasoning. While conventional skills (interpersonal, legal compliance) will always be important for those in public service, principled reasoning is critical when confronting perplexing "right vs. right" decisions (see Brousseau 1998) so frequently encountered today. Table 1.1 outlines a model of ethical decisionmaking.

Before one can reason clearly about ethical issues, it is first necessary to identify ethics-related conflicts. Here it is important to distinguish between an ethical problem and an ethical conflict. An ethical problem involves "a situation with ethical content, requiring individual choices," while an ethical conflict entails "dissonances among principles of right (do good) or among principles of wrong (cause no harm)" (Wartick and Wood 1998: 119). Thus, an example of an ethical problem might be a contemplated action that is right or wrong ("Should I embellish my managerial accomplishments by unfairly claiming credit for the successes of others and scapegoating my personal failures?"). An ethical conflict, by contrast, is more difficult and could involve competing principles of right action ("refrain from sharing privileged information" and "refrain from doing harm to others"), when, for instance, failing to share the information results in avoidable harm (Lewis 1998). A second distinction is between internal and external ethics conflicts. While an internal conflict exists "within the head" of the person himself or herself ("Should I or should I not apply this or that principle or take this or that action?"), an external conflict occurs between two or more persons who disagree about an ethical issue ("I disagree with you that the action I am taking is unethical").

Next, assessment skills are needed to recognize and analyze the ethical issues found in particular settings. It is important not only to distinguish the ethical dimensions of a situation from other overlapping considerations (e.g., legal, economic, technical), but also to weigh a variety of appropriate alternatives and their likely consequences. When conflicts are simple and straightforward, basic skills may be sufficient, but for complex cases advanced skills are needed. Here intuition, luck, and surface knowledge will not be sufficient to resolve tough dilemmas; professional training and development are imperative. It is also useful to have ethics resources available (e.g., ombudsperson, ethics committee, hotline).

Another skill is the ability to say "no" when asked to do something unethical. As simple as that may sound, it is not. It is difficult to tell a superior that his or her instructions cannot be carried out because they may be unethical. It takes a secure person who is aware of his or her core values to refuse to engage in dubious acts.

Empirical evidence exists showing that those exposed to coursework in ethics are better able to withstand pressure from superiors to engage in untoward acts (e.g., Jurkiewicz and Nichols 2002). Dennis Thompson provides wise counsel to public servants by identifying three paradoxes of ethics:

- Because other issues are more important than ethics, ethics is more important than any issue. The central importance of ethics is a precondition for good government and a way to maintain or restore citizen confidence.
- Private virtue is not necessarily public virtue. This paradox distinguishes between personal morality and political ethics cautioning that those in public life must conform to more restrictive standards of behavior (e.g., financial disclosure, post-employment restrictions).
- Appearing to do wrong while doing right is really wrong. Appearances matter even though such standards may be subjective. Those seeking to build public trust, to insure compliance, and to make prudent decisions need to avoid actions that are, or could be perceived to be, unethical. The scandals of the Enron Era add saliency to the relative importance of ethics, the difference between private and public virtue, and that appearances matter (Thompson 1998: 255–57).

Finally, ethical theory can provide insights to guide actions. If higher order moral reasoning skills are important, then knowledge of ethical theory (e.g., consequentialist vs. nonconsequentialist or principle-based vs. casuistic) is crucial to resolving those complex ethical conflicts that call upon advanced skills. Contextual knowledge can be helpful as well. For example, professionals working in health care should be knowledgeable about bioethical issues (informed consent, confidentiality), the clinical setting, institutional characteristics (structure, policies, services, resources), beliefs and practices of patients and staffs, as well as relevant ethics codes and laws that might impinge on decisions (see Aulisio, Arnold, and Youngner 2000). Professional associations like the

American Society for Public Administration (ASPA) and the Council for Excellence in Government have developed general ethical principles for public servants. Familiarity with ethical theories, principles, codes, values, and practices can aid professionals to think through and, hopefully resolve, the mind-bending dilemmas found in today's work environment. Improved ethical decision-making can help to restore citizen confidence and trust in public service.

Leadership Competencies

The third point of the competency triangle is leadership skills. The shift in the environment of public service from hierarchical, bureaucratic, government-run programs to "networks" of goods and service providers from public, private, and nonprofit sectors demonstrates the need for new forms of leadership. Top down, command-and-control styles, while not necessarily a thing of the past, are gradually giving way to collaborative approaches to shared leadership. Leaders need skills in assessment, negotiation, and change management, and these skills can be learned. Regina Blackstone, mentioned at the beginning of this chapter, has the technical expertise required for her research position, but was thrust into a leadership position that called for skills that she had not yet developed. As noted in Exhibit 1.1, leaders of the new public service, such as Regina once she has retooled, will be able to accurately assess, effectively negotiate, and creatively manage change.

Some of the specific leadership competency areas include (a) structural, (b) human resources, (c) political, and (d) symbolic (Bolman and Deal 1991). Skills in the structural category include budgeting, information systems, human resource administration, and planning processes. It is important for professionals to accurately assess the systems in which they operate because they order and ensure continuity in organizations. System dysfunctions can lead to service breakdowns and systems coordination requires mutual adjustments; so in a multisectored, interorganizational, and multijurisdictional environment it is especially crucial to be aware of how various systems function. Leaders need not be technical experts in budgeting, IT, human resources, or planning, but it is important to understand the rudiments of these fields and how decisions are made and how services are provided. While it is more difficult to pinpoint the person in charge of a "network" arrangement often comprising informal project teams, leaders are unlikely to emerge if they lack the assessment skills and managerial acumen to diagnose problems and make things happen in the systems with which they are working.

Next, some leaders are adept in dealing with systems, but lack human resource competencies (e.g., open communication, solid interpersonal relations, and participation-enhancing skills)—a serious deficiency. Leadership involves facilitating, mediating, and negotiating and thereby putting a premium on persuasive powers, good people skills, confidence in others, consensus, and collaboration. No longer can leaders outside of military and paramilitary settings, expect to issue orders to hierarchical subordinates who immediately comply. They must be mindful of amassing facts, articulating goals, working effectively with a range of stakeholders, inspiring trust, cajoling, and embracing public involvement.

Third, it is difficult to overstate the need for political skills—bargaining, resource acquisition, stakeholder relations, and conflict resolution competencies are imperatives when sharing leadership with others. Good interpersonal skills can help in gaining consensus and managing change, but conflict is inevitable when stakes are high and resources are scarce. Knowledge of alternative dispute resolution techniques is often required to resolve conflicts over priorities and strategies and to forge consensus. Facilitative leadership by politically savvy public servants is a glaring need when building alliances, coalitions, and networks with prominent actors and interest groups. Leaders must use their political abilities both within their organizations and in dealings with those outside their institutions if they are to be effective change managers.

Finally, symbolic skills buttress knowledge of systems, people, and politics. These require vision, knowledge of organizational cultures, awareness of institutional routines, and cultivation of collective identity. Leaders need to provide clarity of direction, cultivate shared vision, and evoke inspiration from others. The likelihood of success increases as they become better informed about the: various decision-making processes of collaborating organizations; prevailing values, attitudes, interests, and beliefs of key stakeholders; standard operating procedures of relevant institutions; and extent of loyalty or commitment of employees to their departments and to the routines of their organizations. This requires familiarity with changes occurring in public service because government is privatizing and significant segments of the private sector are "governmentalizing" (Kettl 2000). Unlike the old public service where knowledge of one's own organization—its routines, standard operating procedures, and culture—was often sufficient for success, the new public service requires a broader awareness of collaborating partners operating in different settings.

The leadership skills addressed here barely scratch the surface. A Clinton administration cabinet officer, Donna Shalala, provides additional insights in her top ten lessons for managing a complex public bureaucracy. A number of these are relevant for work in any sector: know the culture of the organization, choose the best and let them do their job, stitch together a loyal team, stand up and fight for the people who work for you, set priorities and stick with them, look for allies where you do not expect to find them, and do not expect to win every time (Shalala 1998: 284–89). Beyond such advice, there are important skills not considered here such as managing for results, facilitating personal and professional growth, and emphasizing citizen service. The chapters that follow will address some of these in greater depth.

Conclusion

The only sure constant in today's environment is rapid change. This fast-paced change poses new challenges for public service. It is no longer acceptable to rely unduly on bureaucratic machines, hoarding knowledge at the top, and dispensing instructions to those lower in the hierarchy to be carried out by protected employees engaging in preestablished routines. This formalistic, static, state-centric approach is outmoded and ineffective in an era of dynamic change. So too are earlier meanings of public service in need of reformulation. A government-controlled merit system is gradually giving way to a new public service. The advent of networks and public-private partnerships has broadened the locus, focus, and skills required of professionals.

The tensions resulting from the interplay of politics and professionalism have ebbed and flowed from the earliest development of public service to the present. Fitness for public service, partisan spoils, and merit have each been ascendant as a criterion for government staffing during different historical periods. The transition from the old to the new public service continues to witness this tension. Political appointees as "citizen servants" work alongside career professionals and both groups collaborate in partnerships with nongovernmental public servants. While political-professional tensions have not abated, indirect or "third party" government puts a premium on politically sophisticated and professionally qualified public servants.

The consummate professional in today's public service requires technical, ethical, and leadership skills. Technical competence helps to ensure that things are done correctly, while ethical competence leads public servants to do good things. Leadership is needed to harness the energies of disparate service providers and orchestrate their efforts to advance the general interest. Citizens will be well served by those servants who possess these skills in rich abundance. However, having the right skill set alone does not capture the essence of public service—commitment to making a difference in the lives of citizens, upholding democratic values, and demonstrating compassion in the service to others. Anthropologist Margaret Mead (2001) said it well: "Never doubt that a small group of committed people can change the world; indeed, it is the only thing that ever has." In the chapters that follow it is important to remember that competency, as important as it is, must be buttressed by a deep and abiding commitment to work for the good of all citizens.

— Chapter 2 —

The Technical Professional
Developing Expertise

Practice does not make perfect.
Only perfect practice makes perfect.
—Vince Lombardi

Technical expertise is one of three hallmarks of a public service professional. Citizens and employees expect service providers and their managers to be skilled in doing their job. If the task is to offer child welfare services, then counselors must understand which types of interventions are most effective and appropriately implemented, how to make efficient use of resources, and how to deal with the inevitable instances when treatments go awry. Because stakeholders demand high levels of technical competence, administrators should be exemplars of excellence. Accordingly, this chapter discusses types of technical proficiency and higher education. It then addresses the rudiments of relevant operational capacities including strategic planning, program management, financial administration, managing people, and information management. The space shuttle *Columbia* calamity, terrorist attacks, the enormous task confronting the Department of Homeland Security, innovative community planning, and unconventional organization charts illustrate and document the analysis.

Technical Expertise

Technical expertise consists of scientific knowledge to understand what to do (e.g., ensuring safe drinking water or space travel), legal strictures governing what should and should not be done (e.g., securing bids for government contracts), and institutional savvy to achieve objectives (such as finding inventive ways to purchase computers).

Scientific mastery is critical because most services (e.g., road construction, emergency management, public health, and information technology) are built on such knowledge. Although many managers do not have a technical background, they must have sufficient, general awareness of such matters to know how to identify those who can bring expertise to bear. Legal sophistication is also needed because laws and regulations provide program standards and guidelines for conduct. They dictate the importance of treating citizens and employees fairly and may specify steps to be taken (e.g., contracting for services or staff). The use of litigation to settle differences further increases the importance of legal facility. Institutional knowledge, finally, is knowing how to accomplish tasks inside an organization. Government agencies, nonprofit organizations, and businesses have formal and informal procedures from buying equipment to getting a definitive answer on a new proposal. Such aptitude includes understanding past practices—why institutions have chosen to do things in certain ways that may make sense when their reasons for them are rediscovered.

Having competency in these three dimensions is a defining feature of professionals. Administrators must have sufficient technical understanding to acquire able personnel and appropriate technology, knowledge of how their subordinates work, and the skill to create financially sound programs. They need to plan program activities, build support from stakeholders, and anticipate opposition. Those who have these talents are positioned to see that programs flourish and have a significant community impact. Achieving success means knowing, adhering to, and applying formal and informal professional standards.

The Road to Expertise

Education continues to play a valuable role in the development of professional attainment by furnishing a crucial baseline for ac-

Table 2.1

Mentoring Program Components

Component	Specific elements
1. Statement of purpose and a long-range plan	Details about activities to be performed; input from stakeholders; needs assessment; operational plan; goals, objectives, and timelines for all aspects of the plan; and funding development plan.
2. A recruitment plan for both mentors and participants	Assessment of expectations and benefits; marketing and public relations activities; targeted outreach based on participants' needs; volunteer opportunities beyond mentoring; and a link to the program's statement of purpose.
3. Orientation for mentors and participants	Program review; description of eligibility, screening process, and suitability requirements; level and type of commitment expected; accountability requirements; expected rewards; and targeted focus for potential mentors and participants.
4. Eligibility screening for mentors and participants	The process for application and review; interviews; reference checks for mentors (e.g., child abuse registry, driving record, and criminal record checks where legally permissible); review of suitability criteria; and successful completion of pre-match training and orientation.
5. A readiness and training curriculum for all mentors and participants	Training staff; orientation to program and resource network; cultural/heritage sensitivity and appreciation training; job and role descriptions; guidelines; confidentiality and liability information; dos and don'ts; crisis management/problem solving resources; communications skills development; and ongoing sessions as necessary.
6. A matching strategy	A link with the program's statement of purpose; commitment to consistency; grounding in program's eligibility criteria; rationale for matching strategy; and pre-match social activities between mentor and participant pools; team building activities.
7. A monitoring process	Meetings with staff, mentors, and participants; a tracking system for ongoing assessment; written records; input from relevant stakeholders; and a mechanism for grievances.
8. A support, recognition, and retention component	A formal kickoff event; ongoing peer support groups for volunteers and participants; ongoing training; relevant issue discussion; networking with appropriate organizations; social gatherings of different groups; and annual recognition and appreciation event.

| 9. Closure steps | Private and confidential exit interviews to debrief: participant and staff, mentor and staff, mentor and participant without staff; clearly stated policy for future contracts; and assistance for participants in defining the next steps for achieving personal goals. |
| 10. An evaluation process | Outcome analysis of program and relationship; assessment of program criteria and statement of purpose; and information needs of stakeholders. |

Source: Adapted from www.ed.gov/pubs/YesYouCan/sect3-checklist.html.

quiring necessary skills, knowledge, and abilities. It offers exposure to:

- relevant social and political trends
- the field's technical language
- the range of skills and standards that modern professionals are expected to possess
- alternative perspectives on issues and problem solving
- ethical norms.

Yet education can do no more than introduce the vocation. It is impossible to furnish the hands-on, capacity-building, and character-forming experiences found on the job (Bok 1986; Bloom 1988). For many the process of acquiring professional-grade knowledge is at least a four-year journey, two in graduate school to gain fundamental information and two in practice to hone specific abilities.

Indeed, most professions resemble a craft in which knowledge and skills are gained through practice with support of others proficient in the field. Consider the following comment from a recent graduate, looking back:

> Well, I know that higher education doesn't cover everything. Overall I'd say that the knowledge, however, I gained was very important. It provided the basis for some things I did after that, and it qualified me for better jobs. But it is true that there was a lot that was not covered in class. From others or sometimes just by figuring things out on my own, I had to learn many things to make my job work. I also had a few people who really helped me and, without them, well, I doubt things would have worked as well as they did.

Education seldom provides this kind of comprehension. Most university internships, for example, are too short to develop genuine expertise.

Postgraduate job experiences, then, involve in-depth learning. Many of these entail unguided, on-the-job experiences insofar as formal training is not always available; those who expect such "advanced training" may be disappointed. For instance, if a handbook of knowledge is available it can be voluminous, vague as to what standards apply, or out of date. Employees do well to take an individualized, proactive approach to meeting their needs. Finding a well-regarded mentor (such as an experienced employee or manager) can be a significant event in one's career. Mentors work closely with new people to help them assimilate the pertinent values, negotiate interpersonal conflicts, overcome technical challenges, and otherwise become productive employees (see Table 2.1 on pp. 36–37 for ideas on how to develop a mentorship program and Emerson 2003 for a description of the U.S. Department of Labor program). Consider this realistic, composite reflection on the part of a hypothetical staff member:

> To be honest, I never thought about finding a good mentor, but I just lucked into a great situation. My supervisor was about ten years from retirement, widely respected and experienced. He quickly became a role model, and I often sought his advice on all kinds of matters. I don't think I ever called him "my mentor," but that is exactly what he was. I cannot begin to tell you how often he covered for me on some of the really dumb things I did during my first year. Well, mistakes are human, and I was lucky that he saw it that way. Anyway, I learned a lot over several years, and he later helped me advance.

Those who take active control over their own learning by seeking all forms of professional development may do better than those adopting a passive, reactive stance.

Notice how such a posture affects the three areas of technical expertise (scientific, legal, institutional). Engineers need to know how to build actual bridges and counselors need to know how to deal with real client problems. What approach works best? Why?

Answers to such questions may be found through mentors, colleagues, and journals, as well as professional association networking. Taking responsibility for one's career ensures that challenges are sought and opportunities for access to others become available.

Likewise, this stance assists in the acquisition of legal and institutional knowledge. Rules and regulations are necessary to ensure compliance and limit liability (Exhibit 2.1). Organizations tend to be unforgiving in the case of those who break rules, but it is sometimes unclear which rules are important and what it takes to excel (as well as avoid trouble). Similarly, institutional wisdom comes from experience that takes time to acquire (a mentor is surely helpful). Because a majority of senior managers in the federal government soon will be eligible for retirement, this knowledge will erode, competence levels may decline, and exposure to corruption will likely increase. Finding ways to retain organizational memory will be crucial, and using retirees in advisory and mentoring roles may be useful. Indeed, each of the three types of technical expertise may already be at risk as shown by the 2003 *Columbia* shuttle tragedy (Exhibit 2.2). In summary, technical expertise requires each of the kinds of knowledge discussed above, and the process of achieving this level of specialization requires graduate education as well as on-the-job experience. Indeed, reflecting the white-collar nature of public service, "Nationally, 50 per cent of government jobs are in occupations requiring specialized training, education, and job skills, compared to just 29 per cent in the private sector" (Walters 2002: 8).

Technical Management Skills

Administrators cannot be entrusted with multimillion-dollar programs unless practiced in the tools and techniques of the profession. The stakes are simply too high, and the public too skeptical. Accordingly, key skills—planning, program management, resource management (financial, human, information)—are briefly reviewed below. These tools are expected to be used in ways compatible with contemporary values such as citizen service, openness and accountability, and high productivity (Holzer and Callahan 1998).

Exhibit 2.1

Technical Expertise: Legal Knowledge

Law is fundamental to professional proficiency: It is inspirational as it sets out basic values or principles that society must follow (e.g., treating individuals with dignity); it provides protections and assurances that help get the job done (e.g., assisting in contract enforcement); it dictates how managers conduct their job (e.g., receiving three bids from vendors), and it furnishes due process rights that managers are required to recognize (e.g., protecting employees from arbitrary administrative actions).

Professionals do well to adopt both a broad and narrow perspective on the law. The broad view focuses on inspirational purposes that provide guiding principles, norms, and values. The narrow view emphasizes specific legal actions that managers must take, and how to avoid legal entanglements (and win those that cannot be avoided). One perspective without the other is fruitless. Understanding the spirit of the law enables the professional to take action when it is unclear and refrain from a search for technical loopholes. Yet such an overall view by itself may be insufficient because specific legal requirements must be ascertained and followed.

It is difficult to give a comprehensive treatment of values found in the law, but some are:

- Respect for the rule of law,
- Respect for the freedom of others to pursue their interests and beliefs,
- Good faith in all activities,
- Fairness,
- Accountability for actions, and
- Respect for human dignity (see also American Bar Association Model Rules of Professional Conduct in Windt et al. 1989).

This list matches widely held values in American society, and this should not be surprising insofar as law tends to reflect social norms.

But specific actions and knowledge of the law matter too. No one wants to become embroiled in legal controversies, yet the potential is clear when dealing with issues such as employee performance,

(continued)

Exhibit 2.1 *(continued)*

supervisory discrimination, contract enforcement, service delivery, access to public information, and contract bidding.

Professionals, then, should expect to deal with legal matters during the course of their careers. Accordingly, it is prudent to be familiar with statutes and cases that have been applied to one's organization (e.g., citizen eligibility for program participation, personnel administration issues, regulatory and licensing procedures) as well as new laws and court decisions that affect citizen, employee, and organizational rights. Furthermore, professionals ensure that administrative procedures are scrupulously followed (failure to do so risks due process violations) and that supervisors act to prevent and correct violations by subordinates. Seek legal counsel before taking action and investigate the availability of agency and/or private professional practice insurance (Wise 1996). Generally, there are two types of justice: procedural (due process) and distributive (fair outcome); ensuring that people are treated in a fair manner enhances the probability that the result will also be fair.

Incorporating the legal dimension into work provides better information and skills to protect citizen, employee, and professional rights and to achieve institutional goals while reducing susceptibility to lawsuits. As Wise points out, "courts have not excused administrators from having to know the judicial interpretations applied to various aspects of administering public programs (1996: 731). Quite apart from legal obligations, public service professionals need to represent the highest values of the nation.

A substantial body of literature exists that discusses the legal system, one that "is not consistent across levels of government, and is not consistently defined for different governmental sectors nor for different types of public officials" (Wise 1996: 713). Various general sources are available (e.g., www.law.emory.edu/erd/index.html; www.nolo.com/) as well as those on liability (Wise 1996; DiNome, Yaklin, and Rosenbloom 1999) and personnel management (Rainey 1997; DelPo and Guerin 2003). HR.com eBulletin examines a wide range of current developments such as pending and recent legislation, case studies, and labor relations. *The Lawsuit Survival Guide* (Matthews 2003) may also be useful.

Exhibit 2.2

Technical Expertise, NASA, and the *Columbia* Catastrophe

The nation's $25 billion space shuttle program was envisioned in the 1970s as the successor to America's moon-landing feats. It depended on relatively low operating costs to offset high development costs. It also set unrealistically high goals, as many as 60 flights a year. And almost from the start, the shuttle program was plagued by design failures, cost overruns, delays, fraud and mismanagement in NASA and its network contractors.

Many of the worst problems were hidden from the public until 1986 when the *Challenger* exploded. Faulty welds—faults that had been concealed through falsified X-rays by a subcontractor to avoid the cost of a repair—had gone undetected until auditors received tips from former employees. Investigators learned that the agency had substantially cut spending on safety testing, design and development, almost from the time the program began. [By contrast] in the [earlier] Apollo project, each component was designed, built as a prototype, and then tested, so when the final system was assembled for a test, scientists had a high degree of confidence that it would work.

But NASA, to save money, decided to cut back on that kind of testing and instead built major components and systems before they were fully tested. Later there were reductions in the ranks of inspectors, and there were failures in the detection of equipment so critical that they might destroy a spaceship. In the swirl of investigations that followed the *Challenger* disaster, it was learned that NASA had misled Congress about costs and schedules, had withheld critical documents and violated Federal codes in thousands of instances. And it had squandered billions of dollars. It turned out that NASA engineers had warned in 1977, 1978, and 1979 that [O-ring] joints of the shuttle's solid fuel rocket boosters were seriously flawed. But the agency took no corrective action. Despite the intense focus on the O-ring problem after the *Challenger* disaster, similar problems were observed on some later *Columbia* flights and those of the remaining three shuttles. [As well] for years, everyone involved in the program worried about

(continued)

Exhibit 2.2 *(continued)*

[silica] tile problems [that cover the vehicle and were the apparent cause of the 2003 explosion].

Tight budgets continue to be a major cause of technical problems, according to engineers and other experts. The difficulties have been compounded by repeated cycles of faulty planning. Other causes include an aging workforce, management shortcomings, and the increasing complexity of projects. In 20 of 28 of its missions, the first in 1981, *Columbia* experienced mechanical or technical problems [causing] more flight delays than any other orbiter. Since *Columbia* was the oldest orbiter, NASA also relaxed maintenance standards, an acknowledgment that an old machine cannot perform as well as a newer one. Numerous reviews have concluded there are systemic weaknesses in the shuttle program that go deeper than the mission-by-mission problems. NASA staunchly denies safety has slipped.

Sources: Excerpted and condensed from McFadden (2003)—Copyright © 2003 The New York Times Co.; and Flaherty et al. (2003)—Copyright © 2003 The Washington Post. Used by permission. See also Columbia Accident Investigation Board (2003) for withering criticism of three decades of failure to reconcile the cost, schedule, and safety goals of NASA.

Planning

An organization is the structure through which goals are accomplished. To organize is to determine the relationship of people or departments to each other (i.e., who is responsible to whom, and for what?). To plan is to decide what gets done. It also involves determining which people or departments are best to ensure that work is accomplished and that those involved are provided with the necessary resources. These are daunting tasks as shown in two cases involving domestic security.

Few managers have the opportunity to design a large agency *de novo*. In the aftermath of the 9/11 terrorist attacks, the 70,000-employee Transportation Security Agency was quickly created to ensure air travel safety. Deciding which departments—and the interrelationships among them—should meet multitudinous objectives is a substantial task. Even after planning and goals setting, formidable questions remain: How will technology needs be met? What sources of intelligence will be used and how will they be coordinated? How can cooperation with foreign governments be achieved? Similar questions pertain to the Department of Homeland Security (DHS) established a year later. The agency, with a staff of more than 170,000, is composed of over 20 preexisting departments (totaling 80 personnel and pay systems) each with its own organizational culture. Many employees remain concerned about losing their jobs, taking pay cuts, and having no protection against partisan pressures (they all lost civil service tenure when transferred to the DHS)—and one-third of all federal personnel are considering leaving government (Kaufman 2003). Called the "ultimate management challenge" (Blair 2002), only the future will tell if a cohesive department can emerge to secure the nation's borders and transportation infrastructure. In 2003, five senators released a "report card" giving the agency a "D+" in meeting its goals (Mintz 2003).

The crux of planning, then, is to identify goals and resources, and to ascertain how and when resources are used to accomplish objectives. Strategic planning is a technique used to define the major purposes and specific activities of an organization (Bryson 1995; Kaye and Allison 1997). Such planning can be undertaken by just a few managers, or used to solicit the input of hundreds of employees, thereby increasing openness and shared decision making. It is a stepwise process that first requires organizations to define their mission (what is our purpose?) and vision (what do we want to become?). Then, institutions take inventory of major defining challenges and opportunities in their environment, as well as the unique strengths and weaknesses that affect how well they can respond. Against this information, goals are put forward and selected that best further the mission and respond to the challenges and opportunities identified. Finally, for each goal agencies establish specific objectives and workable strategies to achieve them. Thus, strategic planning is a process that clarifies the mission and provides specific strategies for achieving goals.

Such planning is an important, widely used technique. In the late 1990s, three-quarters of cities with populations over 50,000 utilized it in at least one of their departments within the past twelve months (Berman and West 1998). The agency director or senior managers lead the activity, but it involves many departments and offices. Each unit has information to contribute, and they frequently participate in strategic planning through employee teams. Many senior managers prefer a participatory process because it increases employee commitment and the quality of the result. Exhibit 2.3 discusses a modified approach to strategic planning known as community-based strategic planning.

Goals may not be well defined as legislatures often enact broad rationales and goals without specific purposes or methods for accomplishing them (e.g., social services are funded to address drug rehabilitation, but often lack mention of the type of services offered or the level of outcomes to be achieved). The necessity for clear goal setting also occurs because agencies experience a plethora of competing—and conflicting—demands and priorities. Interest groups, citizens, other organizations, and elected officials are apt to express contradictory views. For example, should drug treatment programs target teenagers or working mothers? Should treatment centers be located in low- or high-income areas? Should faith-based therapeutic interventions be used? Should funds be shifted from prevention to rehabilitation—or the reverse? Should services be available to those outside the service area? Should they be privatized? The lack of a clear plan can lead to "mission drift" and "goal displacement," if objectives are not focused on the intended aim.

Resource availability further mandates planning, as it affects spending priorities. Managers have limited time and staff. They are responsible for many different aspects of their programs, from personnel recruitment to quality control to interdepartmental coordination to community relations. They have to plan when to do what and who will do it. Government services can be provided more economically by the private or nonprofit sector—and vice versa—depending on policymaker ideology, bureaucratic inertia, or empirical evidence.

Exhibit 2.3

Shaping Communities

Strategic planning is employed to redirect organizations toward new strategic missions. But it is also used to help guide communities. Many important problems transcend the capacities of individual departments or cities; they require a joint, coordinated approach among many agencies and cities. Examples include pressing community issues such as drug use, traffic congestion, environmental protection, school performance, illiteracy, joblessness, and communicable diseases.

Community-Based Strategic Planning (CBSP) involves multiple agencies and jurisdictions. It is initiated typically by elected officials, who can command legitimacy in dealing with broad public issues and can furnish necessary resources. Leaders from other organizations are invited to participate. Because the actual plans involve offices and departments within these different organizations, department heads and program managers participate as well. Such planning typically requires three to six months, in large measure because of difficulty of scheduling meetings, research that may be required, and the need to discuss in both formal and informal settings how to coordinate efforts.

Economic development provides an example. Some cities were bypassed by the social, economic, and technological progress of the 1980s that brought prosperity to others. One such jurisdiction is Hollywood, Florida (population 139,000). Its appearance in the 1980s was as it was in the 1950s; there had been little progress over the years. In the early 1990s, the city undertook CBSP with commerce, government, banking, higher education, tourism, and neighborhood development; a public-private partnership was later established as well. Today, downtown Hollywood is a thriving, rejuvenated regional destination that boasts distinctive shops and nightlife, along with new parking garages and apartments.

The success of CBSP has not gone unnoticed abroad. To increase economic development in Eastern Europe and deal with the effects of sustained environmental degradation, the U.S. government and the European Union are subsidizing CBSP in regions of Slovakia, Serbia, and Herzegovenia.

Program Management

Planning is also done at the program and individual level. For instance, one useful tool is a timeline or "Gantt" chart, which specifies each activity of a program, tracks its progress and when it is scheduled to finish—a few months to several years, depending on the nature of the project (Ammons 2002; Frame 2002). It also shows the current status or phase of each project, insofar as some activities occur early in a project and others take place toward the end.

After managers have decided program goals and objectives, what functions are needed to achieve the aims (e.g., field support, scientific assessment, information technology management), who is responsible for ensuring that different tasks are fulfilled, and what support capabilities and resources are at the ready? What is the quality and quantity of these resources? What collaboration is needed between programs? What adjustments may be required? Such questions apply to, for example, a homelessness program. Activities may include health screening and maintenance, assistance with other agencies, job training and job search monitoring, and so on. Then, managers determine if functions (e.g., access to medical facilities for health screening, database of clients), staffing (quantity and quality), and resources are available. Finally, synchronization between activities and personnel is required (e.g., a client's medical condition may affect her job skills and search efforts).

While internal organization is important, external relations also matter. Programs must build and maintain support among stakeholders, funding organizations (including other governments), elected officials and boards, and the public. A homelessness program, for instance, will need to ensure that outside groups view it as effective. Program coordination challenges are evidenced in federal environmental protection where 29 different agencies have responsibility for clean air, safe water, and solid waste management. Collaboration in other areas is required as well: early childhood programs (11 agencies and 20 offices), economic development efforts (342 programs), and job training (40 different programs)

Exhibit 2.4

9/11 and Local Emergency Management

Although the federal government is charged with heading up the response to large events such as wars and disasters, most crises are handled at the state and local levels. Indeed, just as New York residents would normally call their local 911 number for fires, medical emergencies, and rescue needs, residents relied on their city government in the wake of the two plane crashes. The tasks of response and recovery were immense after the building collapses:

- Setting up a command center because the planned hub of operations had been in the World Trade Center itself,
- Restoring communications that had been ruptured by the attack,
- Providing a sense of order amid the chaos of the catastrophe,
- Securing the city from further aggression,
- Evacuation of approximately 25,000 alive, injured, and dead in the buildings plus evacuating approximately a half million people from lower Manhattan,
- Setting up medical facilities for the many who were injured and furnishing morgues for the dead,
- Offering a vast array of disaster services such as temporary housing, medicines, clothing, counseling, hotlines, and insurance and claims assistance, and
- Coordinating all these efforts among a vast network of agencies, levels of government, and individuals.

Despite the enormity of the events and setbacks—the horror of the acts of terrorism, the unprecedented collapse of super-skyscrapers, and the loss of the emergency command center itself—New York City responded heroically. Mayor Rudolph Giuliani acted as the chief local coordinator, the national communicator, and an individual comforter at countless funerals. Police Commissioner Bernard Kerik directed the successful evacuation efforts of lower Manhattan. Deputy Fire Chief Peter

(continued)

Exhibit 2.4 *(continued)*

Hayden commanded the immediate evacuation of the twin towers after the loss of the fire chief. They later all commanded the cleanup of Ground Zero in which 1.2 million tons of debris were removed in less than four months. Transportation Commissioner Iris Weinshall and Transit Police Chief Michael Ansbro supervised transportation for those evacuating the area.

Meanwhile, Governor George Pataki declared the site a state disaster and quickly got a federal disaster designation. The Federal Emergency Management Agency provided a door-to-door relief effort. Congressman Jerrold Nadler introduced the Public Safety Officer Benefit Program (to compensate the families killed in the line of duty), which was signed into law in three days. U.S. Senators Hillary Clinton and Charles Schumer negotiated federal access to $20 billion for local rescue and recovery efforts. These efforts were in support of local leadership, which so brilliantly rose to the occasion despite the enormity of the calamity and the extraordinary task of coordinating so many systems amid warlike conditions (Cohen, Eimicke, and Horan 2002).

The issues involved in preparing for likely (e.g., cyclical acts of nature such as hurricanes and tornadoes) as well as completely unforeseen (e.g., terrorist strikes or meteor crashes) crises are immense: stockpiling resources, coordinating specialists (e.g., medical, emergency response, public safety, and scientific personnel), and providing plans for coordinated response. These concerns supersede technical matters, and raise ethical and leadership challenges to prevent crises, maintain a sense of urgency, and to respond to those problems that occur—difficult tasks because the likelihood of a crisis occurring during any one administration may be low.

(National Commission on the Public Service 2003). Similarly, at the local level, emergency management responses to the 9/11 attacks illustrated the difficulty of coordination and the crucial importance of technical, plus ethical and leadership, competencies (Exhibit 2.4).

The significance of good organization cannot be overemphasized. Once a project is organized, it becomes possible to accomplish goals by determining how tasks get done, and how well they get done. Project employees depend upon one another to achieve mutual objectives. Because personal understandings and relationships tend to persist—regardless of outcomes—ongoing planning is important in reassessing the importance of different goals as well as finding leaders who can help people and their projects adjust to new needs.

Managers have basic tools that can assist them in organizing. The organization chart identifies functions, who is responsible for them, and who is accountable to whom. It may be a hierarchical pyramid, a matrix format (people or units reporting to more than one unit), or star-shape (every unit reporting to the same center). It can also show working relationships among organizations. In any case, it is a telling reflection of management philosophies. Some agencies have turned the traditional pyramid chart upside down with executives at the bottom in support of the entire institution, much like a coach both sustains and leads a sports team. Figure 2.1 presents an unconventional, circular chart.

The process flowchart, another tool, specifies tasks, their duration, the persons involved, and the order of completion. In the past decade, rethinking process flows ("reengineering") has been attempted to improve business, public, and nonprofit management (Linden 1995). Work can be designed so that citizens deal with a single point of contact—"one-stop shopping" programs—to reduce time and frustration. They require that frontline employees be empowered to deal with multiple aspects of the job and be responsible for coordinating work. Increased use of information technology has also changed work processes, in large measure because data are available to more people who are empowered to make decisions.

Finally, contracts with nonprofit and private organizations to perform work extend the organization beyond the formal boundaries by allowing managers to draw on others to achieve goals. This does not release administrators from responsibility to ensure that the work is performed (Osborne and Plastrik 1998). Officials sometimes have advisory boards to ensure community support.

Figure 2.1 **Organization Charts**

Traditional model

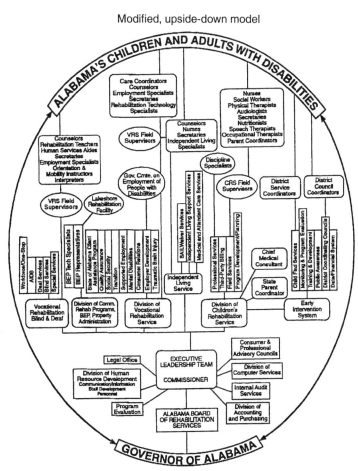

Modified, upside-down model

Source: Alabama Department of Rehabilitation Services, Customer Support System (2001).

They also speak to local organizations to maintain such support, and ensure that funding sources are well informed.

Resource Stewardship: Money, People, and Information

Deciding what needs to be done, and then getting it done, is the essence of management. However, an equally important matter is to ensure that the necessary resources are in supply to get the job accomplished. Without money, people, or information—and each requires considerable technical expertise—little will be achieved.

Money

The budget is a statement about the level of resources available to each department or program during each period. The politics of budgeting is the process whereby departments, organizations, and/ or policymakers negotiate requested funding; the practice of budgeting is as much about technical analysis (how to justify a proposed request) as it is about negotiating skills (how to acquire what is needed). The complexity of budgeting occurs not only because there are different types of budgets (for operating and capital expenses), but also because each year involves different budgets (planning for next year's expenditures, spending this year's allocations, and accounting for last year's outlays). In addition, managers rely on more than just allocation of general taxes to pay for programs; some depend on user fees, bonds, and/or grants from other organizations. State and local government agency directors, thus, require knowledge about creating special tax districts, such as community or downtown development, libraries, schools, water management, public health, or neighborhood beautification. Public organizations also often do as much grant writing as nonprofit organizations. Clearly, professionals need to know about raising money, as well as spending it.

Money is closely related to accountability. People want to know (a) that dollars are being used as intended and (b) what they are getting for their taxes. The first concern addresses issues of fraud and abuse; most public organizations have extensive controls and restrictions to ensure that spending is appropriate. Still, ethically questionable practices occur. For example, Orange County, California, invested some of its funds in high-risk stock market activities in the mid-1990s; when these investments turned sour and losses were exposed, the public was rightfully outraged. In Seminole County, Florida, tax collectors in 2002 provided knowledge of pending foreclosures to their friends and families enabling the purchase of property deeds at very attractive prices. Such cases do not necessarily indicate legal wrongdoing, but they are morally dubious and highlight the need for vigilance.

Accountability for program outcomes is a second concern. Historically, most budgets accounted only for expenditures appropriately spent; today budgets are often complemented with performance measures that detail specific program results (Coplin and Dwyer 2000; ASPA 2000). For example, a revenue program can gauge the number of taxpayers, those who do pay, and those who should be penalized for not paying. These indicators can be compared over time and provide information to program managers and elected officials.

People

Although people skills are often contrasted with technical skills, they too include technical knowledge. No matter how good one is in dealing with others (a judgment best made by someone else), employment relations offer scientific, legal, and institutional challenges in recruitment, training, compensation, and termination, as well as employee rights and responsibilities (Berman et al. 2001).

Recruitment begins with a position description: the responsibilities and competencies required for the job (before recruitment occurs, however, organizations also do a technical job evaluation to assess the position and determine its compensation). The subsequent interview process focuses on the candidate's technical knowledge and past work experience; casual queries about nonjob-related matters may be discriminatory and should be avoided (e.g., maiden names, religion, race, social clubs, arrest record, child care arrangements, credit history). A final step involves reference and background checks, a process also infused with legal implications such as character defamation and negligent hiring. Once selected, training and development is important to ensure productivity. One problem occurs when technically proficient people are promoted to supervisory roles without appropriate training (Conlow et al. 2001; Belker 1997); such supervisors may be deficient in supervision skills (see Exhibit 2.5 on pp. 56–57).

Managing people also involves technical issues of setting compensation rates, dealing with benefit packages, and conducting employee evaluation. Employee compensation can be based on different philosophies reflecting employer beliefs that salaries should be below, at, or above market. Technical expertise in setting compensation rates, dealing with benefit packages, and doing performance reviews is critical. It is important to note that modern managers have become increasingly savvy about the legal rights of employees. When staff does not meet expectations, "progressive discipline" begins with verbal suggestions for improvement followed by written reprimands. Providing substantiation is important because most career public employees have due process rights and cannot be terminated without just cause, and private sector workers can sue for "wrongful discharge," that is, the employer violated an implied or written contract or public policy protecting employees refusing to do something that is illegal.

Finally, people have other rights as well, but may be limited by the employer's right to workplace efficiency. For example, they have freedom of speech but voicing dissatisfaction to the press without exhausting internal processes first may result in disciplinary action. Likewise, employees have religious freedom, but they may be required to work on religious holidays. Of course, organizations do well to make reasonable accommodations to maintain positive labor relations. Employees also have a right to privacy; employers cannot intrude into their private life or workplaces. However, organizations may adopt policies that permit searches of all departmental property.

Information

If people are to do their jobs well, then they must possess the necessary information. The need for effective information management is especially pronounced when multiple agencies and jurisdictions work together to administer programs (e.g., the management of environmental resources or the conduct of modern warfare).

Decisions about what information to share are part of the planning and program management issues discussed above; they flow naturally from decisions about what gets done. But the management of the technical infrastructure for disseminating information is a relatively new function in some agencies. Indeed, the multimillion-dollar (and sometimes billion-dollar) infrastructure must be professionally managed and staffed. Many agencies now have a chief information officer who sets the policies, advises agencies on investment decisions, and oversees staff ensuring that the agency's networked systems are up to date and fully operational. The staff of central information technology departments also provides support to units and users who purchase and maintain equipment.

This is a dynamic field: Information technology issues change quickly, and range from system reliability, connectivity, and computer viruses to system access and data security. The only certainty is that future issues will be different and challenging, and thus demand professionals with the technical expertise to address them.

Conclusion

Citizens expect public servants to be professional, which, in part, requires having the technical knowledge to do their job effectively. They need to know scientific skills, legal rules and regulations, and institutional operations, which are acquired through education and experience. While the profession of management is several generations old (before the 1950s, management of organizations was regarded as "common sense"), it generally lacks certification requirements (although the masters of business and

Exhibit 2.5

Dealing with a Poor Superior

Because supervision involves many skills, it can be deficient in some areas. There are numerous "how to survive the bad boss" resources (Deep and Sussman 1992; Di Nino 1996; Brown 1987). Some managers:

- fail to give clear instructions ("I shouldn't have to tell you what your job is"),
- are inconsiderate of one's professional opinion ("I will tell you what you do, not the other way around"), or
- are uncaring about your time ("I know it is Friday, but I need this done by Monday morning").

Others are inconsistent in their praise and recognition, give accolades based on nonjob-related criteria (e.g., those who curry favor with the boss), or fail to give positive feedback and recognition ("Why should I have to tell you that you are doing a good job?"). Still other supervisors enjoy putting people down, sometimes in public ("You have ruined almost every assignment given you"), or lack initiative to execute the department's mission ("I can't do this without explicit authorization").

Such behaviors are troublesome, not only because of what they cause, but also because of what they do not cause. First, they reduce motivation and initiative, resulting in tasks that employees do not do. Second, they deprive supervisors of information about their program; activities that might be undertaken are not even identified. Third, supervisors with a "troublesome" reputation will fail to attract and retain superior staff. Applicants have choices and may go elsewhere. Even when hired, they may soon depart, thus depriving the program of talent and experience.

What can be done? It does little good to complain to peers; employees get sympathy but still face the same superior. It helps little to blame that individual's personality because that is difficult to change. It may not be useful to suggest supervisory training because many organizations are focused on results, not the quality of supervision. Nonetheless, here are some suggestions:

(continued)

Exhibit 2.5 *(continued)*

- employees should avoid doing obvious things that bring negative consequences (e.g., not meeting deadlines) (Cohen and Eimicke 2002),
- employees may need to adjust their own styles to that of the supervisor,
- employees cannot use poor supervision as an excuse for lowering their personal standards,
- employees should focus on behaviors that they do want from their supervisors, rather than on personality.

Finally, when nothing can be done, employees need to keep a cool head and consider moving on. While supervision clearly requires professionalism, the way people deal with it is a reflection of their own professional standards.

public administration degrees, which emerged in the early 1970s, may be viewed as surrogates). However, postgraduate certifications are available.

The Certified Quality Manager examination, which is similar to the SAT and includes several essay questions, was created in the mid-1990s by the American Society for Quality. It is a formal peer recognition that an individual has demonstrated proficiency and comprehension of the pertinent body of knowledge (Table 2.2). The technical skill set includes understanding standards and concepts, knowing how to implement organizational assessments, and maintaining a customer focus in support of organizational goals. Because such subjects are relevant to many areas, it is no surprise that the program has generated considerable interest outside of the quality profession (Hutchins 1997). The International City/County Management Association also has a voluntary testing program. University extension services in many states provide classroom training under the auspices of the Certified Public Manager program. Finally, noncredit certificates in nonprofit management can be earned at over thirty institutions of higher education (M. Lee 2003).

Table 2.2

American Society for Quality: Certified Quality Manager Body of Knowledge

Body of knowledge	Handbook for Quality Management chapter
Leadership	
Organizational development	I B, C
Organizational culture	II B
ASQ code of ethics	VII A
Techniques for facilitating/managing organizational change	II E
Conflict resolution techniques	VII A
Team process	
Team formation and evolution	VII E 1
Team facilitation techniques	VII F 1
Team reward and recognition	VII F 4
Strategy development and deployment	
Environmental analysis	
Legal and regulatory factors	II G, III A
Stakeholder groups	III F
S.W.O.T. [strengths, weaknesses, opportunities, threats]	III H
Customer/employee surveys and feedback	IV C, D
Internal capability analysis	IV C
Strategic planning and assessment	
Strategic planning techniques and models	III A
Formulating quality policies	III B
Deployment	
Assure integration between strategic and other plans	III B
Metrics and goals that drive organizational performance	III F
Quality management tools	
Problem-solving tools	
The seven management and planning tools	VI A 2
Root cause analysis, plan-do-check-act and other like models	VI A 3
Tools for innovation and creativity	I A, VI A
Cost of quality	VI B
Measurement: assessment and metrics	
Process goals	I B
Process capability	VI A
Benchmarking: internal and external	V A 6
Customer-focused organizations	
Customer relationship management and commitment	
Customer service principles	IV C, D, G
Multiple customer management	IV H
Supplier performance	
Supplier selection strategies and criteria	I D
Techniques for assessment and feedback of supplier performance	I D

Management
    Principles of management
        Total quality management   I
        Organizational structures   II B
        Business systems and independence of functions   V B
    Communications
        Communication techniques   II D
        Information systems   VI A
        Knowledge management   VIII A
Projects
    Project justification and prioritization techniques   VI B, A, V A
    Project planning and estimation   VI A, V A
    Monitor and measure project activity   V B
Training/development
    Alignment with strategic planning and business needs   VIII A
    Training materials and curriculum development   VIII B
    Techniques for evaluating training effectiveness   VIII D

Source: Adapted from www.qualityamerica.com (retrieved May 10, 2003). Used with permission from QualityAmerica.com.

To conclude this chapter, technical expertise emphasizes what should be done, not why it should be done. Thus, it produces an interesting paradox: the greater the demand for technical proficiency, the greater the demand for ethics and leadership—the topics of the next two chapters.

— Chapter 3 —

The Ethical Professional
Cultivating Scruples

In matters of style, swim with the current.
In matters of principle, stand like a rock.
—Thomas Jefferson

Ever since George Washington required "fitness of character," service to country has been regarded as more than a matter of mere technical skill. Competence also included personal honor, a view shared by Theodore Roosevelt who believed that, "To educate a man in mind but not in morals is to create a menace to society." This component of the "professional edge"—excellence in ethical bearing as well as technical ability—has long been a hallmark of governance. The obligation and privilege to uphold this ethos remain in today's multisectored public service. When representing the state, governmental, nonprofit, and business officials alike are stewards of the common good. The concern for ethics, then, is founded upon the capacity of government (and its agents) to exercise power, a function that is moral in nature insofar as policy decisions are the authoritative allocation of societal values.

Accordingly, public servants must not only do technical things right but also do ethically right things. Leaders without basic ethics skills are professionally illiterate. This is what makes the execrable corporate, not-for-profit, and governmental scandals of recent years so devastating—the worst form of incompetence does not involve not knowing how to do something, but rather not knowing why something is done. Many professionals in a variety of fields—management, law, securities, policy, accounting, banking—have demonstrated a lack of understanding of this fundamental precept. Muriel Siebert, the first woman appointed to the New York Stock Exchange, explains the emblematic episode:

> I basically feel that Enron was a case of total moral bankruptcy. It was not just the company and its executives. It was not just the accountants. They had to get legal opinions from a law firm. They had to get the derivatives (i.e., a security or financial asset, such as an option or futures contract, whose value depends upon the performance of an underlying security) from banks and Wall Street firms. One group alone could not have done it. The money was vast, and the money was fast. (Holdstein 2002)

The centrality of ethics in management in all sectors of the economy is undeniable. It is not an imposition or constraint, but the foundation of everything a professional is or does.

Because controversy is inherent in decision making and there is "no one best way" to deal with ethical quandaries, professional practice requires that moral criteria be integrated into policymaking. What is needed is not only technical ability to analyze problems but also the capacity to grasp those problems in a manner consistent with professional rectitude. Yet professionals may be unprepared to deal with conflicts between ethical values (e.g., honesty, integrity, promise keeping) and nonethical values (wealth, comfort, success).

FBI agents not heeding terrorist warnings, firefighters setting fires, questionable Red Cross fundraising and blood safety practices, clergymen abusing children and their superiors covering up the problem, preemptive war making, Olympic judges rigging scores, stock analysts giving biased ratings, and corporate officers "restating" record numbers of audits all demonstrate that ethics is key to the identity and legitimacy of any organization. In the last case, for instance, "the core purpose of accounting is, after all, to verify authenticity, to certify to the public the integrity of the accounts of a business or public agency" (Frederickson 2002: 9). Instead these professionals, unlike hospital financial officer James Alderson (Exhibit 3.1) who uncovered the largest Medicare scandal in history, sacrificed the independence they claimed to possess.

Exhibit 3.1

**Hundreds Knew But Did Nothing;
One Person Did Something**

*Our lives begin to end the day that we become silent
about things that matter.*
—Martin Luther King

James Alderson was an unassuming financial officer for a hospital in northwest Montana. Yet he would blow the whistle on the fraudulent Medicare practices of one of America's largest hospital conglomerates, Columbia/HCA and one of its subsidiaries Quorum. His actions would lead to the uncovering of the largest Medicare scandal in U.S. history. For Alderson, the decision to undertake the arduous fight was based on his determination to fulfill his professional duty and personal ethics.

From 1984 to 1990, his professional life was uneventful. "It was a late September afternoon in 1990, about two months after Quorum had assumed management of the hospital . . . Mr. Alderson was meeting with a consultant who helped prepare the hospital's government cost report when Clyde Eder, a Quorum administrator, stepped into the room. Mr. Eder asked the two men whether they usually prepared two cost reports. They were uncertain what he meant. "I said, 'No, we just prepare one cost report,' the consultant recalled. "I thought he was talking about maybe preparing one for Medicaid and a different one for Medicare."

But Mr. Eder meant something quite different. Quorum submitted aggressive cost reports to the government, claiming the largest possible number of expenses. But in case a later audit rejected those claims, the company also assembled a second set of more conservative reports for its internal use. Several days after the awkward encounter, Alderson was informed that he been dismissed. In 1992 he started conducting legal research in a local library and drafted a letter outlining his lawsuit. It accused Columbia/ HCA Healthcare Corporation and Quorum Health Group of defrauding the Medicare program and other health insurance

(continued)

Exhibit 3.1 *(continued)*

programs—a case that would involve more than 200 hospitals in thirty-seven states. There could be little doubt that preparing multiple sets of cost reports was a nationwide practice engaged in by numerous professionals.

By 1997, there were raids of Columbia/HCA hospitals in six states and the FBI arrested several executives. On October 2, 1998, the Justice Department accused Quorum and Columbia/HCA of these wide-ranging charges:

- filed claims and received reimbursement for nonallowable costs such as for marketing, advertising, and unrelated investments by mischaracterizing them
- billed Medicare for idle space in hospitals by claiming it was being used for patient care
- concealed overcharges and Medicare auditing errors that favored HCA facilities
- shifted costs to home health rehabilitation and other facilities that Medicare reimbursed at higher rates.

By the end of 2002, a tentative settlement was reached requiring HCA to pay the Justice Department $631 million. Previously HCA paid $250 million to resolve other cost report issues, as well as $840 million to settle other whistleblower cases and criminal fines. As one official said, "James Alderson had a solid belief that this was wrong and a determination to do something about it. It's a truly amazing example of how one [individual] can make a difference."

Source: Adapted from Ventriss and Barney (2003).

"Ethics," then, is not something mysterious and far removed from ordinary life; instead, it is about people making decisions every day. There is no doubt that everyone encounters ethical dilemmas; the only question is when and whether they are ready.

What is needed is a management approach to the subject that includes understanding why people behave the way they do. To assume anyone with good character can act honorably in professional situations is no more sensible than suggesting that someone can function as a physician without special training. While values are imprinted at an early age, the real question is how they are applied at the workplace. Professional socialization can equip leaders to anticipate problems, recognize when they occur, and provide frameworks for thinking about issues; it affects not only ethical awareness but also moral reasoning and behavior (Rest and Narvez 1994; Menzel 1997; Menzel with Carson 1997; Bruce 1996). Without this preparation, individuals may rely on technical proficiency (in fact, doing things right can become a dominant *moral* code), unexamined personal preferences, passive obedience to authority, and/or unquestioned organizational loyalty. Those serving the public may bring idealism and cynicism to their work. This chapter aims to reinforce the former and minimize the latter by briefly defining values and ethics, and then examining (1) professionals and moral development, (2) individual ethics, and (3) organizational integrity.

Values and Ethics

The most important thing in life is to decide what is important. Values are what matter to someone; they describe who he or she is. They shape one's worldview and clarify the character of the individual and ultimately the community; shared values are a kind of "cement" that brings and holds people together. Exhibit 3.2 displays universal and democratic values (for professional values, see Exhibit 1.1). Conflicts are inevitable, even desirable; governance is about maintaining conditions in which civilization is possible. Indeed, the Greek root for ethics is *ethos*, which emphasizes the perfection of the individual and the community in which he or she is defined.

Ethics is the way values are practiced. As such, it is both a process of inquiry (deciding how to decide) and a code of conduct (a

Exhibit 3.2
Universal and Democratic Values

Universal Values

In the late 1990s (Kung 1998), 6,500 representatives from a wide variety of world religions reached agreement on a global ethic; a council of former heads of state and prime ministers then ratified the statement. Delegates from both groups articulated two universal principles: Every individual must be treated humanely and every person and group must respect the dignity of others. These foundational principles lead to commitments to a culture of: nonviolence and respect for all life, solidarity and a just economic order, tolerance and truthfulness, and equal rights and partnership between men and women. Global standards emerged from another international gathering (Kidder 1994): love (compassion), truthfulness (honesty), fairness (evenhandedness), freedom (pursuit of liberty), unity (the common good), tolerance (appreciation of variety), responsibility (care for self, the community, and future generations), and respect for life (reluctance to kill). See also the 1947 United Nations Declaration of Human Rights. For a report on emerging public management standards in a transnational world see Cooper and Yoder (2002).

Democratic Values

Democratic values in the American context have a minimum of six major elements. At least two are fairly universal among all democratic societies throughout history. The first is the belief in systematic governance that enables various issues to be brought into the public domain (or sent out of it) through an authorized process. A second value is representation, which is the belief that a system of elected representatives should decide upon the major policy questions affecting the public good. This is important because direct democracy is rarely feasible except in limited cases such as town halls and miscellaneous voter referenda.

A third value of American democracy is the division of political power in a federal system: horizontal separation of the powers

(continued)

Exhibit 3.2 *(continued)*

of the national government into three branches checks the power of any one branch by the other two, and vertical separation divides power between the national government and the states. A fourth significant democratic value is the protection and celebration of individualism. In particular, the Bill of Rights protects numerous personal rights such as the freedoms of speech, press, and assembly, freedom to bear arms, freedom from military billeting, unreasonable search and seizure, self-incrimination, and double jeopardy, rights to due process, a speedy trial, legal counsel, and a jury trial, among others.

A fifth firmly held right is religious choice. Separation of church and state ideally functions to protect the individual's freedom of religion without making religion a universal way of life. Finally, while it is often unrecognized as such, a sixth American democratic value is the pursuit of a relatively pure form of capitalism. This is a creed to have the least government intervention possible, while still providing—and therefore balancing issues leading to—a stable, humane, and safe environment. Thus while American society allows and encourages income disparities based on individual initiative and market mechanisms, it discourages system distortions such as insider trading or information monopolies.

Specific administrative values flow from some of these democratic values. There is a general understanding that public managers should implement policy but not usurp the process or amass power themselves (serve and facilitate rather than preside). There is a belief that they should be efficient and effective with the public's resources (conservation). There is a credo that administrators should support the citizens' right to know the public's business (openness and transparency). A similar value is that managers should support the public's right to be involved in governmental business through forums such as public hearings, citizen surveys, focus groups, and advisory boards.

set of standards governing behavior). Ethics is a system of right and wrong and a means to live accordingly. It is a quest for, and understanding of, the good life. Grounded in values and predicated upon ethics, professional responsibility demands the discretion of practitioners. But upon what foundation are decisions made?

Professionals and Moral Development

The key theory of moral development was formulated by Lawrence Kohlberg (Table 3.1). This hierarchical, inclusive taxonomy posits that individuals develop moral maturity by moving gradually from stage to stage in each of three levels:

- Preconventional level moral reasoning reflects punishment avoidance (Stage 1) or an instrumental orientation (Stage 2); the person is self-interested and either fears or uses others.
- Conventional level thinking regards right behavior as conformity to expectations of significant others (Stage 3) or allegiance to the broader social order (Stage 4); the person's point of reference is a group, either small and personal or large and political.
- Postconventional judgments are derived from the moral autonomy resulting from critically examined values in the social contract upon which the social order is constructed (Stage 5) or from adherence to transcendental ethical principles (Stage 6); the individual is an independent actor as moral precepts trump the social expectations found at level two and the self-interests in level one.

Growing from level one to level two is a common, though not inevitable, psychological development requiring little deliberation. Stages are not skipped, and evolution can stop at any point. Actual reasoning tends to reflect one dominant stage, although it may sometimes occur at one stage higher or lower. Kohlberg believed that most people are at the conventional level because the postconventional level requires an uncommon commitment and contemplation.

It is fitting, therefore, that professionals strive to make decisions at the highest level of moral development. They cannot form

Table 3.1

Kohlberg's Stages of Moral Development with Behavioral Orientation

Level	Self-perception	Stage orientation	"Right" behavior	Reference frame
Preconventional	Outside group	1. Punishment and obedience	1. Avoid punishment; defer to power	1. Physical consequence of actions
		2. Instrumental—relativist	2. Satisfaction of needs	2. Human relations are like a marketplace
Conventional	Inside group	3. Good boy–nice girl	3. That which please/ helps others	3. Majority or "natural" behavior
		4. Law and order	4. Duty, maintenance of social order	4. Authority and fixed rule of society
Postconventional	Above group	5. Social contract	5. In terms of individual rights, free agreement	5. Constitutional/democratic agreement, social utility
		6. Universal-ethical	6. Choice of conscience, ethical principles	6. Universal imperatives, justice, human rights

Source: Adapted from Kohlberg (1971: 164–65). Copyright © 1971 Elsevier. Used with permission.

judgments solely from the self-interested level-one perspective. Level-two thinking also may be inadequate because some social roles are unjust (e.g., law enforcement officials in the Jim Crow U.S. South; physicians in Nazi Germany). Level-three reasoning, however, prevents abuse of professional skills for one's own advantage or for that of one's social group. The idea is not to deny self or collective interest, but to temper them in light of a higher claim of human dignity (Snell 1993). Professionalism, in short, requires dedication to technical and ethical excellence. It is unthinkable for the professional to do otherwise when grappling with important problems.

The Professional and Individual Ethics

Approaches to Ethics

The essential issue of ethics is, as Socrates said, "What ought one to do?" However, no unified theory, no one secular approach, resolves all moral dilemmas. In deciding what to do, it is likely that people have always considered potential outcomes of their decisions and/or relevant guidelines to tell them what is right. It follows that cognitive schools of thought generally contend that matters of right and wrong are a function of either:

(a) the expected results of an action (consequentialism or teleology) or
(b) the application of pertinent rules (duty ethics or deontology).

In consequentialism, the best decision results in "the greatest good for the greatest number"; what is right is that which creates the largest amount of human happiness. In duty ethics, however, certain actions are inherently right (truth telling) or wrong (inflicting harm), irrespective of supposed consequences; one must see one's obligation and do it. Actions are to conform to moral rules. In deciding what rule to apply, one asks, "Would I want everyone else to make the decision I did?" If the answer is "yes," then the choice is justified; if "no," it is not.

The claimed strength of these approaches to ethics is that they are superior to an intuitive understanding of right or wrong—to say nothing of sheer expediency. In weighing expected results, the decision maker acts as an engineer calculating the costs and benefits of an action; in choosing among rules, she plays the role of a judge. Yet these theories have undue confidence in the power of reason: predicting consequences in human affairs is hazardous and choosing among conflicting duties is daunting. Moreover, both can be seen as rationalistic efforts that ignore the person making the decision. Ethics involves more than following general norms such as consequences or duty (Bowman 2003). Since antiquity, people have also relied upon their personal characters when confronted with dilemmas.

In this theory, known as virtue ethics, the primary faculty is moral intuition, not intellect. Reason may be essential in decision making, but the source of morality is human sentiment. Ethical questions are not simply technical ones to be resolved by projecting assumed results or established rules to a situation. Virtue ethics, instead, is a way of life, not merely a method of analysis. It is about right character more than right procedure. Indeed, reason easily leads into error insofar as many do not have the capacity or training for discursive reasoning (consider the convincing—and opposing—jury closings on *The Practice* or *Law and Order* television courtroom dramas).

This school of thought, accordingly, is a more personal, subjective approach to morality than cognitive ethics. Answers to questions of "What to do" have little to do with results and rules, and everything to do with what kind of person one is. An individual must *be* before he can *do*. Personal character is forged through experience by developing praiseworthy habits. The role of theory is not to get the professional out of a jam, but to help build one's fiber. Excellence in character ensures that the professional has "the right stuff" to do the right thing at the right time.

Yet no general theory of human virtue exists; virtues seem to vary from time to time and place to place as some virtues may not apply to all (e.g., men vs. women, young vs. old). Further, the virtue school lacks a theory of action. Virtues may generate instructions for action (the virtue of justice, for instance, provides the motivation to act justly), but what does a just person do in a given dilemma? The theory, finally, lacks integrity; one may be good but not know how to do good. Worse, confusing the two can easily lead to self-righteousness; if one believes he is good, then it is not hard to think that what he does is good.

The Ethics Triangle

If philosophers cannot agree on competing models (results-and-rules cognitive approaches and virtue ethics), then why should public servants? The reason is that they must be able to defend their judgments: professionals, by definition, are obligated to develop virtues, respect rules, and consider results. A decision-making tool, the "ethics triangle" (Svara 1997), recognizes the complementarity and interdependence of the imperatives in these three schools of thought. It emphasizes that cognition without virtue is as insufficient as virtue without cognition (Figure 3.1).

Each point of the triangle provides a distinct filter to clarify and reframe different aspects of a situation. Operating inside the triangle helps prevent the shortcomings of each approach as its angles inform and limit one another. Consider these examples:

- exaggerating advantages of a proposal to secure support
- insisting on one's own way at the risk of unit cohesiveness
- cutting corners in established processes
- showing disloyalty when times are tough
- concealing errors
- engaging in favoritism
- failing to report violations of agency policy
- denying responsibility for a mistake

Considering the results point of the triangle, "the greatest good for

Figure 3.1   **Ethics Triangle**

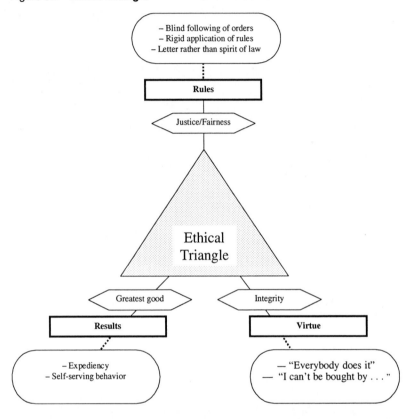

Key: ( ) = Examples of nonethical or unethical behavior or attitudes resulting from narrow application of the approach.
   Source: Adapted from Svara (1997: 39).

the greatest number" is achieved by refusing to engage in these
actions because of the negative consequences from their exposure.
Using a rules-based interpretation, the duty to avoid such behavior
is clear. Under virtue ethics, finally, excellence in individual and
community character is nourished by doing the right thing in each
case.
   Here is an actual case that occurred during the buildup for the
2003 attack on Iraq:

A few months before I retired from the military, part of my responsibility was to submit monthly Unit Readiness Reports (URRs) to higher headquarters. Unit commanders are responsible to ensure that their units are combat ready 24/7. They must maintain 80 percent or greater readiness every month; how they get there is entirely their responsibility. I discovered that every month the number of soldiers trained and passing physicals was increased. When the URR numbers are less than 80 percent, commanders and staff would paper drill ("pencil whip") selective training events that never took place. I mentioned to the commander that the numbers were incorrect; his guidance was "we'll make it up next month." The unit had recently had a mandatory military ethics class instructed by the commander himself. When the reports were submitted to higher headquarters with the commander's signature and one of the staff members, I refused to sign them. (anonymous personal communication, February 1, 2003)

Like the hypothetical examples earlier, the ethics triangle can be helpful in analyzing how to deal with this situation.

More complex issues—such as the genuine ethical dilemma below—produce more interesting, sometimes conflicting, findings.

Bob has heard from his manager that their organization's staff will be downsizing; it could be as little as 5 percent or as much as 30 percent. However, the supervisor told Bob that "we're all under strict orders to keep it quiet" so that the agency's best employees will not seek other jobs. Ron, one of the finest professionals in Bob's unit, upon hearing downsizing rumors, told Bob that he was sure that he could get another job at a new business if a reduction in force occurred. However, their openings will close soon. Ron asked Bob, "Will there be layoffs?" (Bowman and Williams 1997: 522)

Generally speaking, when considering the results point of the triangle, the critical question is, "Which decision has the most utility in serving the greatest good for the greatest number?" In contemplating duty-based ethics from the rules part of the triangle, the key question is "What decision best carries the weight of universality?" (i.e., "What if everyone did that?"). Finally, from the virtue ethics angle, one might ask, " Who am I?" "What would a person of integrity do?" or "How can I best achieve excellence in this circumstance?"

Although the synthesis developed from triangulation analysis does not tell one what to do or how to do it, it offers guidance about how to handle the situation:

- Because all schools of thought in the triangle imply that confidential information is to be respected, an honest answer to Ron's question might be, "I don't know what the level of reduction will be, but some reduction will occur. Ron, I want to keep you and help you, but you must decide what to do."
- Given that duty and virtue ethics emphasize truth-telling, the fair treatment of individuals suggests that the information Bob has should not be withheld, especially for organizational convenience and expediency; it follows that Bob should tell Ron what he has heard.
- Because credible arguments hold for the above options, the deliberations stimulated by the triangle could elicit moral imagination, which seeks a solution that both respects privileged organizational information and honors individuals. That is, promoting an ethical department through open communication could assist Bob in dealing with his manager (a discussion limited to rumors is insufficient) while demonstrating personal integrity (to tell Ron, but not the entire staff, is improper). Accordingly, Bob could tell Ron that he himself has heard rumors, too, and that he will seek clarification from his superiors—the only ones that can provide such information.

This analysis, then, is useful in teasing out the underlying logic by which actions are justified.

Of course, none of these strategies will satisfy everyone, but that is hardly the point; the triangle cannot produce a final, perfect decision for all seasons. Instead the decision-making process highlights a key function of ethical management: generating alternative viewpoints, systemically evaluating them, and crafting a considered judgment. The result is not a muddled compromise but a conscious attempt to reconcile conflicting values. This is difficult to do, and that is why these decisions are not easily made.

This eclectic technique for adjudicating matters of right and wrong is very demanding. Yet in light of the shortcomings of each point of the triangle, there is little alternative; such an ethic is necessary given the complexity of the human condition. When choices are guided by benevolence, creativity, and an ethic of compromise and social integration—a moral tenet of democracy—there is at least the satisfaction that the problem has been fully examined and that the result can be rationally defended.

The goal is to strive for balance; governance is not geometry, but the art of the possible. It is an imperfect world where no one gets all he or she wants. In ethics, as in the rest of life, there are no magic answers. Differences between theories, nonetheless, should not lead to despair or the conclusion that one is as good as another. Better to have an imprecise answer to the right question than a precise answer to the wrong question.

Indeed, a narrow, overreaching application of a single approach at the extremes of the triangle (Figure 3.1) at the expense of the others holds considerable dangers: expediency (consequentialism), rigid rule application (duty ethics), and self-justification (virtue ethics). Attempts at rationalizing the eight dubious behaviors listed at the start of the subsection illustrate these risks. Instead the task is to consider the issues from each viewpoint and make an informed judgment. Professionals can do no less. Ethical quandaries are maddeningly intractable—and hauntingly unavoidable. Still if they cannot be conclusively resolved, then that only demonstrates how fundamental they are; the fact that decisions are hard does not stop them from being made.

The ethics triangle, then, like a good map, offers choices, not formulas. Just as a map outlines a journey, the triangle provides help in making the inevitable compromises. As Aristotle admonished, do not expect more precision from the subject matter than it can allow. Professional ethics is more like an art than a science; instead of expecting definitive technical solutions, an aesthetic perspective appreciates that conflict is essential and productive. "Great art is beautiful precisely because of tension, not in spite of it" (Anon. 2002). Like the artist, the professional creatively com-

Exhibit 3.3

Organizational Ethics in the Nonprofit Sector

Bonnie Feinman, founder Special Families (San Diego, California), with Levi F. Robinson and Bruce Hillman

American society was created with a basic distrust of government, and that suspicion remains as a large part of the national culture. As a direct result, these 1.5 million nonprofit arts, environmental, human services, civil rights, and other organizations have gained considerable power and respect; because they do not distribute profits, they are exempt from taxes by virtue of being organized for public purposes. They not only provide services, but also promote such values as community justice, compassion, and social responsibility. Given their altruistic purpose, many people do not question the behavior of these organizations. This public reverence is matched only by outrage at such scandals as:

- exorbitant salaries paid to United Way of America (and some other nonprofit) executives in addition to a series of highly publicized fraud cases;
- overhead expenditures twice the average for charitable organizations on the part of the U.S. Olympic Committee; and
- chronic quality control problems, fundraising and distribution inefficiencies, as well as a diversion of substantial 9/11 funds for administrative purposes on the part of the American Red Cross.

Indeed, the general assumption that nonprofits promote ethical conduct, the public's limited attention span, and a willingness to forgive obfuscates the need for ethical training in the third sector. In addition, important barriers to the incorporation of ethical values in daily operations include the following:

- Compliance with legal constraints and regulations, and publication of an admirable mission statement are often regarded as sufficient.
- A pluralistic staff, representing multiple professions (each with their own ethics code) establishes a territorial attitude

(continued)

Exhibit 3.3 *(continued)*

> that may support conflicting standards, a situation that complicates identification of common values.
> - Performance is judged by volunteer board members with a business, bottom-line orientation.
> - An attitude that because staff members must deal with "difficult" populations, nonprofits "earn" a tolerance for less than exemplary management.
> - Tight budgets common to nongovernmental organizations restrict dollars available for training.

Leadership is, of course, a significant factor in setting an organization's moral direction. In one example, a nonprofit agency serving emotionally disturbed children had CEOs with a social work background for most of its 100+ years of existence. With rare exception, the social work ethos carries a moral dimension that places the highest priority on helping people. Beginning in 1990, the required professional background of the CEO changed from social work to business administration.

With this change came a shift in focus: The first priority was the bottom line, which took on a moral dimension because only then could children be helped. This had a domino effect on decisionmaking throughout the staff as the agency took the "low road" to organizational ethics. The primary question for personnel issues, program planning, and daily childcare decisions became: "Is this cost effective?" rather than, "Is this helping a child?" Licensing regulations were regarded as necessary evils; the goal was to avoid fines and bad publicity. Quality standards were something to prove to the accrediting organization with the proper documentation. Other nonprofits were regarded as competition and offers of collaboration were regarded suspiciously. Given this perspective, the organization represents Kohlberg's Stage 2 of moral development.

With uneven accountability, access to donated funds, and a client base comprised of the neediest members of society, the potential for abuse cannot be overlooked (e.g., see Exhibit 4.5 on the United Way of America). The first step in advancing ethical

(continued)

Exhibit 3.3 *(continued)*

behavior is creation of clear ethical guidelines. Beyond that, there must be institutional encouragement of ethical behavior so that the principles behind the guidelines become an accepted part of the agency's ethical infrastructure. It is not enough that these organizations were created to do good work; they must do good work in an honorable manner. Because the nonprofit sector avoids much of the regulation and scrutiny found in business and government, it must develop and apply its own standards; if it avoids its responsibilities, its very purpose for existence is negated.

bines differing influences. The need for judgment is not eliminated, but rather the triangle enables the skilled management of ethical ambiguity and independent thinking.

Organizational Ethics

Individual-centered ethics is necessary, but not sufficient, for understanding the full scope of professional ethics. Because employees are susceptible to workplace influences, organizations are also important (recall the Greek emphasis on the citizen and community). People may make judgments based on personal standards, but institutions define and control the situations in which decisions are made (see the discussion of the nonprofit sector in Exhibit 3.3). That is, organizations are major agencies of social control; ethical behavior is not only a psychological phenomenon but also a sociological one. As Myles's Law of Bureaucracy dictates ("Where you stand depends upon where you sit"), what employees ought to do is affected by their organizational roles.

Some resist acknowledging institutional factors for fear of diluting personal moral responsibility, but this concern is based on a false dichotomy. Recognizing the role of organization does not exculpate wrongdoers; it simply recognizes that "no man is an island," and that both the individual and the collectivity of which he is a part share important obligations. In order for either one to exercise responsibility in an informed manner, their interdependence must be seen and acted upon (see Exhibit 3.4).

Kohlberg's six stages of individual moral development, in fact, can also be applied to organizations. Stage-1 institutions focus on survival as their moral beacon; any strategy will be employed to ensure it. Those in Stage 2 define success by manipulating others; victory justifies the tactics used. Stage-3 companies, nonprofits, and public agencies conform to the practices of peer institutions; prevailing industry customs dictate what is right and wrong. Stage-4 organizations take direction from legitimate authority to determine standards; their moral compass is based on society's legal structure. Units representing the next stage rely on tolerance, open discussion, and participatory management in upholding—or changing—the social contract under which they operate; standards are derived through critical analysis and consensus. Finally, Stage-6 businesses, not-for-profits, and governmental departments profess ideals such as justice and individual rights; balanced judgment among competing interests, based on universal principles, determines right behavior. When laws violate these principles, principles ultimately prevail.

For purposes of analysis, these stages can be condensed into two organizational approaches (see Exhibit 3.5 on p. 82). The personal, negative, punitive, "low road" compliance strategy derives from Kohlberg's lower stages. This policy is clearly important, for without it a comprehensive ethics program may lack credibility. Yet it concentrates on individuals, defines ethics as staying out of trouble, emphasizes "symptom-solving," and often uses ethics to control behavior instead of to encourage improvement. If this approach represents the lowest common denominator, then the "high road" strategy symbolizes the highest common denominator. A structural, affirmative, commitment system based on the more mature stages of Kohlberg's framework is aimed at deterring rather than merely detecting problems by promoting right behavior. Instead of stressing blame and punishment, the approach focuses on reform and development. A robust ethics strategy, described below,

Exhibit 3.4

Individuals, Organizations, and Self-Inflicted
Negative Interdependence

A too frequent destructive pattern in organizations goes like this: The manager sought, for reasons of career advancement in the internally competitive environment, to devolve as much responsibility for mistakes as possible onto the project managers. They, in turn, were doing the same with the technical professionals. The lower-level workers, then, had a strong need to conceal problems from superiors for as long as possible. This led to late "discoveries" of problems, followed by too hasty efforts to correct problems, with everybody trying to protect his or her reputation, which often further slowed and clogged the policy process. All the players understood what the problems were, at least from their point of view, but they also knew that these issues could not be safely discussed openly because it would be read as an admission of timidity or incompetence on the part of those who went public.

The core issue was that the organizational structure, with its system of internal hierarchy and competition for power, impeded discussion of what was interfering with successful coordination. The negative relationships had themselves been established as responses to pressures to maximize competitive individual performance. The chief victims were not only "burned-out" workers, but the sense of trust among colleagues in a common enterprise, a trust whose lack was costing the organization dearly in its own standing with its constituents. The collective learning capacities of the agency were being actively short-circuited by social and moral, not cognitive, factors, especially the zero-sum, adversarial relationship between higher and lower levels of the hierarchy as well as among coworkers. These problems had, however, remained invisible from the point of view of the formal organization.

In other words, the agency was suffering from self-inflicted negative interdependence. To escape this, it needed to reform structurally so that interdependence created among those working together could be recognized and supported to produce positive outcomes. Effecting this change would not be without costs. It

(continued)

Exhibit 3.4 *(continued)*

would require instituting more job security, flattening the hierarchy of control, and setting up a team-oriented, rather than indi-
vidually focused, system of competitive rewards. In addition, the
managers would have to reorient their activities to promote mutual trust through continuous sharing of information.

All these developments require a qualitative change of attitude
throughout the organization. These advances could be expected
to pay off by avoiding bottlenecks in coordination and burnout.
To work, however, the reorientation would at the same time require top management to act in good faith with its employees, by
entering into relationships as a fully accountable participant rather
than as a distant controlling force. One could hazard the predic-
tion that whether management will actually affect these changes
is very likely to be decided by their sense of the surrounding social climate: whether it is stable and cooperative enough to allow
the agency the time and space it would need to institute such far-
ranging reforms.

will likely include elements of both plans, although not necessarily in equal proportion.

Creating an ethical institutional culture is no more easily achieved
than resolving individual moral conundrums (White and Lam 2000;
Trevino et al. 1999; Gilman 1999). In an organizational age, instruments of leadership are often corporate in nature. Indeed, the cor-
nerstone of a comprehensive ethics program is a code of ethics. While
their value is certainly arguable (see Exhibit 3.6 on p. 83), codes
can play significant aspirational and operational roles when seen as
a means to a larger end. The real issue is how these documents are
developed and what goes with them in order to make them meaningful in daily management. Like any organizational initiative, the
impetus to create (or reinvigorate) an agency code must have authentic leadership support. The actual strategy, produced and implemented by a representative employee taskforce, begins with a
self-generated needs assessment to gather information, encourage

Exhibit 3.5

Comparing Organizational Strategies

Low road

>   Ethos: Conformity with external standards
>   Objective: Prevent criminal conduct
>   Leadership: Lawyer-driven
>   Methods: Training, limited discretion, controls, penalties
>   Assumption: People driven by material self-interest

High road

>   Ethos: Self-governance according to chosen standards
>   Objective: Enable responsible conduct
>   Leadership: Management-driven
>   Methods: Education, leadership, accountability
>   Assumption: People guided by humanistic ideals

Source: Adapted from Paine (1994: 113).

participation, conduct workshops, and create a shared vocabulary. Depending on the results, the initiative could include:

- advice mechanisms and reporting channels (e.g., establishing an independent advisory ethics board available to all, grievance procedures, toll-free whistleblower numbers [see, e.g., www.hotlines. com], support structures to ensure due process, an ombudsman)
- decision-making tools (e.g., rotating appointments of an "angel's" advocate tasked to raise ethical issues in staff meetings, or formulating "ethical impact statements" prior to major decisions)
- promotion activities (posting of the code in the department, as well as reprinting it in agency newsletters and reports; recognizing exemplary cases in an awards program)

Exhibit 3.6

Debating Codes of Ethics and Conduct

Standard affirmative arguments contend that codes:

- acknowledge the moral character of democracy
- honor transcendental ideals of self-government
- provide a symbolic basis for public expectations
- inspire moral behavior in public service
- offer a "shield" of protection for employees
- furnish a frame of reference to legitimize the discussion of workplace ethics.

Standard negative arguments maintain that codes:

- lack utility because they are either too vague (aspirational codes of ethics) or too precise (legal codes of conduct)
- contain contradictory provisions and/or have no priorities among them
- foster the official hypocrisy and public cynicism that they are designed to prevent, if not enforced
- focus on employee obligations to the employer to the exclusion of organizational responsibilities to foster ethics
- emphasize proscribed, at the expense of prescribed, behavior.

- personnel system changes (revising recruitment, training, and performance evaluation processes, including identification of ethical dimensions of jobs in position descriptions and whistle-blower protections against retaliation)
- periodic ethics audits (conducting document reviews, vulnerability assessments, employee interviews and surveys, evaluations of existing systems) to provide an ongoing appraisal of program effectiveness.

The objective is to make the code a living document by offering opportunities to participate in its development and evolution, infusing its values into the routines of the organization, providing procedures for its interpretation, and ensuring its enforcement.

While it may be true that little of importance occurs without individuals, little is lasting without institutions. Thus a good place to start is to:

- change the chief executive officer's title to the chief ethics officer,
- hook up an ethics hotline in her office,
- increase executive exposure to criminal and civil liability,
- include outside directors on nonprofit and business boards,
- create "open book" management systems,
- rotate auditors on a periodic basis,
- strengthen conflict-of-interest rules,
- adopt a "three strikes and you're out" corporate death penalty (revocation of corporate charter with the third criminal conviction), and
- support calls for a national commission on white-collar crime.

What is needed, in short, is an actual commitment to an ethical infrastructure rather than just an announcement about an actual commitment. Indeed, one Defense Supply Center employee believes, "Each organization is different and has diverse motivations. We should ask ourselves if ethics initiatives are more for public relations than for establishing an ethical organization. For those of us who have been around for a while, and watched programs *du jour* come and go, one develops a healthy skepticism about the intentions of organizations" (anonymous personal communication, January 26, 2003).

While no strategy will be without criticism, if all proposals are rejected until perfection is guaranteed, then improvement is unlikely. Public and private organizations should plant and cultivate standards by which a professional can measure his or her behavior, encourage correction of deficiencies, and minimize institutional conditions that lead to unethical behavior. The issue is not whether norms of conduct will develop in an organization, but rather what they are, how they are communicated, and whether all are fully conscious of the ethical dimensions of work. The idea is to nourish a transparent institutional culture by offering incentives for ethical behavior, reducing opportunities for corruption, and increasing the risk of untoward conduct.

Like the top of a jigsaw puzzle box, such an initiative can provide a point of departure and serve as an enabling device to strive for professional ideals. It must have the leadership's dedication, be "home grown" by employees themselves, and include a clear policy statement, explanatory guidelines, due process procedures, and employee training, as well as sanctions and rewards. That is, there must be top-down commitment to, and bottom-up participation in, processes designed for continuous improvement. Such a program makes common rationalizations of questionable behavior (e.g., "What I want to do is not 'really' unethical" or "Because the idea will help the organization, I will support it") much more difficult (Gellerman 1986). Organizations, paradoxically, are at their most dangerous when they are successful because people become arrogant and that prevents learning. In the absence of an ethics initiative, business-as-usual expediency and an "anything goes" mentality is likely to dominate, condoning untoward behavior, reinforcing amorality, and discouraging ethical action.

Conclusion

This chapter, after defining values and ethics, discussed moral development theory and the strengths and weakness of three major approaches to ethics—results, rules, and virtue—as part of the mosaic of understanding moral philosophy. Because individual professionals must justify their decisions, the ethics triangle, which emphasizes the interdependence of these approaches, was presented and used in case studies. As Stephen K. Bailey (1965) believed, the dilemma—and glory—of public service is to be consistent enough to deserve respect from others (and oneself) and pliable enough to accomplish ethical objectives.

Ultimately, the challenge of every public servant is to resolve to act solely in the public interest and to shun the many opportunities that threaten this resolve. The quest to improve social circumstances, to fulfill human potential, is to lead the good life. The state of mind required to achieve this is eloquently described by Max Weber:

> [I]t is immensely moving when a mature person . . . is aware of a responsibility for the consequences of his conduct and really feels such responsibility with heart and soul. He then acts by following an ethic of responsibility and somewhere he reaches the point where he says: "Here I stand; I can do no other." That is something genuinely human and moving. . . . In so far as this is true, an ethic of ultimate ends and an ethic of responsibility are not absolute contrasts but rather supplements, which only in unison constitute a genuine person—a person who can have the "calling" for politics. (Carney 1998)

Insofar as the whole point of leading organizations is to recognize the vitality inherent in conflict and to harmonize pressures in praiseworthy ways, attention then shifted to organizational ethics. Moral development theory was applied and condensed to delineate components of an ethical infrastructure. Such programs can reinforce an exemplary organizational climate, but they cannot create it—that remains the function of leadership, the subject of the next chapter.

— Chapter 4 —

The Consummate Professional
Creating Leadership

*The leader must know, must know that he knows,
and must be able to make it abundantly clear
to those about him that he knows.*
—Clarence B. Randall, private sector executive

Public service professionals confront "wicked" and complex challenges on behalf of society (chapter 1). They need to possess an array of technical competencies, subject-matter expertise, operational planning skills, and functional management proficiency in areas such as program management and human resources (chapter 2). They also should have a finely honed ethical facility to balance the starkly competing interests so common in public settings (chapter 3). Although these talents are necessary, they are not sufficient for true leadership. This chapter explores the complexities and subtleties of this key human phenomenon. The crucial nature of leadership is demonstrated by the organizational vulnerability created in its absence (Exhibit 4.1).

Leadership is a challenging subject, full of platitudes as well as sophisticated models. It varies significantly over time and from one situation to the next (Bass 1985, 1990) and involves a sequence of assessment and goal-setting competencies, personal characteristics (traits and skills), individual styles, leader behaviors, and critical evaluation. A leader's assessment of the organization includes evaluating institutional dynamics and the external milieu, while also assessing the constraints faced in carrying out routine functions and unique changes. This creates a context for establishing priorities and a leadership agenda. Because people come to leadership situations in diverse stages of readiness, their

Exhibit 4.1

Leadership and The Nation's Information Infrastructure

One of the most crucial aspects of domestic security is the nation's information infrastructure. This vast nervous system of networks, servers, databases, software and communication lines controls our transportation and financial systems, food and power sources, commerce and public health systems, government services, and so much more.

Remarkably, the Bush Administration has devoted little leadership, staff, resources and attention to this important segment of the homeland security mission.

The problem of cybersecurity is real. The White House concedes this in its "National Strategy to Secure Cyberspace." The report says, "A spectrum of malicious actors can and do conduct attacks against our critical information infrastructures. Of primary concern is the threat of organized cyberattacks capable of causing debilitating disruption to our nation's critical infrastructures, economy, or national security." So far, the administration's efforts in this area have been marked by instability and turnover in the top ranks of the federal cybersecurity community, suggesting a lack of focus and resolve. Since December, a slew of highly regarded and dedicated cybersecurity officials has left. In addition, the cause of cybersecurity is plagued by staffing and resource shortfalls. The government's national cybersecurity center consists of hundreds of critical—but vacant—positions. All this in the wake of regular audits by OMB, the General Accounting Office, and federal inspectors general that find agencies woefully vulnerable and ill prepared for cyberattacks.

Source: "Leadership Is Needed" (2003: April 28). Reprinted with permission from ATPCO.

personal characteristics are a large part of that preparedness. While no absolute set of qualities is necessary for all situations, certain traits and skills tend to be more important than others. Traits are inherent properties and part of one's personality, while skills are learned. This is not to say that traits cannot be enhanced through training or that some people do not have natural gifts.

The individual also brings a style to situations, a dominant pattern of behaving in a position. Styles, like characteristics, are expressed through behaviors toward tasks, people, and the organization. Thus a four-star general's leadership style varies from that of a nonprofit executive, which in turn differs from the talents needed by a CEO of business competing for public contracts. Indeed, the required skills for the same role fluctuate over time as the internal needs and the environment of the organization changes. Finally, the leader has a responsibility to evaluate the effectiveness of actions taken (Figure 4.1). This final evaluation overlaps with the initial assessment phase, thus beginning the cycle of leadership again.

To illustrate these aspects of leadership, a case study (based on Riccucci 1995) of the most expensive scandal of the twentieth century is analyzed as part of the chapter narrative. The Savings and Loan (S&L) crisis of the late 1980s–early 1990s was actually a series of debacles that "made a few people preposterously rich and will leave most of us significantly poorer" (L.J. Davis quoted in de Leon 1993: 135). The fiasco involved incalculable costs, but simple dollar accounting, according to the U.S. General Accounting Office, was estimated to be over $500 billion (de Leon 1993: 130). Although a final figure may never be known, the costliest bailout in American history will be paid by the American taxpayer (for an update, see Labaton 1998). Not only is the episode interesting on its own merits, but also it proved to be a prelude to the continuing scandals in today's Enron Era, which is discussed in the next chapter.

The professional exemplar profiled in the case demonstrates the ideals discussed in this book: technical skill, moral courage, and leadership ability. He assesses a hostile environment, plans goals and backup strategies, refines his traits and skills, varies his style to suit evolving situations, displays the full gamut of management behaviors, and evaluates what occurs. He is also a useful example because he moves from business to the government and back several times, but that does not change his public service orientation. Sometimes he is cloaked in the formal authority of governmental

Figure 4.1   **Leadership Components**

The leader assesses organizational, environmental,
and individual constraints, and then sets personal
and organizational goals.

⇓

Personal traits and skills are used.

⇓

The leader uses his or her style range
to select behaviors to emphasize.

⇓

The leader acts in three major domains:
task, people, and organization.

⇓

The leader evaluates organizational
as well as personal effectiveness.

positions, but other times he has no more than professional dedication as both a lawyer and accountant addressing concerns of the
populace. Finally, he illustrates that most public professionals work
in relative obscurity, even though he has probably saved taxpayers
between one and two hundred *billion* dollars. Yet Bill Black, former

deputy director of the Federal Savings and Loan Insurance Corporation, does not do it for profit, fame, or power. He does what he does because it is a job he loves, he is dedicated to service, and he considers his contribution to the commonweal fit reward.

Assessment and Goal Setting

In the cycle of leadership, assessment of the organization logically comes first. This is clearest with new leaders who conduct reviews of work systems by scrutinizing data and interviewing people. Assessment, like all leadership activities, is a cyclical process conducted on a regular basis. Effective executives have the analytic ability to review large amounts of information and sift out important trends. Areas to be examined are task skills, role clarity, innovation and creativity, resources and support services, subordinate effort, cohesiveness and cooperation, organization of work and performance strategies, and external coordination and adaptability (Yukl 1998). The types of questions to be asked in assessing organizational readiness for high performance are posed in Table 4.1.

The Savings and Loan Calamity: Leader Assessment, Constraints, and Goals

The 1980s were the best of times and the worst of times. America had been awakened to the need to restructure its economy due to a series of financial shocks incurred in the 1970s from shifting international geopolitical markets (in oil) to loss of market share (e.g., in automobiles, electronics, and manufacturing). Major improvement initiatives such as Total Quality Management were launched to address product quality and customer service. However, the decade was also one of decadence and self-indulgence as mergers and marketing became icons of easy success and extravagant lifestyles. The most infamous example was the S&L debacle, which ultimately cost (and is costing) the taxpayers one-quarter of a trillion dollars ($1,000 per person in the nation).

Table 4.1

An Organizational Effectiveness Audit

Major organizational factors to assess

Task skills: Do employees have the skills necessary to do their jobs? Do they have the training and supervisory feedback to perform with excellence?

Role clarity: Do people know exactly what is expected of them? Do teams and committees work well, even without direct assignments? Are there aspects of organizational work that are not done because no one takes responsibility for them?

Innovation and creativity: Does the unit/organization adopt new state-of-the-art methods quickly? Does it innovate? Does the organization allow all types of employees to be innovative and creative?

Resources and support services: Does everyone have the resources they need? Are the pay, benefits, and work policies adequate to compete in the market? Are there administrative personnel to support employees in areas such as human resources, budgeting, and information technology?

Subordinate effort: Do most employees work hard? Is there a sense that the unit/organization's business must not be neglected?

Cohesiveness and cooperation: Is there a sense of cooperation in the unit/organization? Are labor relations typified more by a sense of harmony than hostility?

Organization of work and performance strategies: Is work organized in a way that maximizes efficiency? Are employees provided incentives to do excellent, rather than just mediocre work?

External coordination and adaptability: Does the unit/organization have effective ties to its external constituencies? When the external environment shifts suddenly, does the organization react deftly?

Although the problem was partially created by unusual economic conditions fueled by historically high interest rates, the concern here stemmed from public leadership in many quarters that either took advantage of the situation or steadfastly ignored the looming crisis because it was an expensive nuisance that was best shunted off to someone else's "watch." Following were among the culprits:

- a Republican president unwilling to address an expensive issue he inherited,

- a Democratic house speaker bent on protecting white-collar criminals from his state, as well as a group of senators ("the Keating Five") on both sides of the aisle ready to intervene for a big-dollar contributor,
- a Congress incapable of passing any sensible regulations to protect either individual depositors or the public purse, and
- a business community self-righteously claiming profits for themselves and declaring any losses to be a governmental responsibility.

So pervasive was this public-private conspiracy that it is impossible to find a hero in a prominent public figure; the only leadership provided was by the administrative staff personnel. They fought for the laws, tools, and resources to correct a problem that grew tenfold during the 1980s because corruption and greed was allowed to flourish in the privately owned—but publicly insured—thrifts.

One such person was Bill Black, a man who started as the head litigator for the Federal Home Loan Bank Board (FHLBB) in 1984, and later became the deputy director of the Federal Savings and Loan Insurance Corporation (FSLIC). His external assessment began during his successful prosecution of a Florida thrift when he defended the Board in a lawsuit. He saw firsthand how corrupt savings and loan (S&L) presidents would try to defer government receivership as long as possible so that they could squander millions of dollars without personal liability. His view was that the regulators had the skills, role clarity, motivation, cohesiveness, and ability to perform efficiently. However, they would have to be aggressive in coordinating with external groups (especially political actors), creative in finding new strategies to uncover massive fraud and insolvency, and capable in securing the means to deal with a problem quickly spiraling out of control.

The constraints were substantial. Congress expanded deregulation, restricted regulatory intervention, and cut budgets in the vain hope that thrifts would "grow their way out of the problem." Further, while regulators are relatively powerful in legal authority, both the

Office of the President and the Speaker of the House curtailed their position power and resources at every turn. Finally, Black's leadership experience was largely lacking when he took the position.

The goals of Black, and his first boss at the FHLBB, Edwin Gray, were not merely routine in nature. Although they did have to continue the S&L investigations and takeovers, they wanted to resolve a national scandal. The FHLBB and Black had to work with the legislative branch to formulate policy, to acquire resources, and to get relief from political intervention in prosecution of flagrant corruption. This would take incredible courage (more case installments follow).

Trait and Skill Competencies

Like a soldier going to war, a leader must have not only a battle plan, but also talents and skills to draw upon during the conflict— the second leadership aspect (Figure 4.1). For the first fifty years of the twentieth century, researchers studied traits and skills of leaders in order to determine which were most important. Ralph Stogdill (1948) and others concluded that a theory of traits and skills was insufficient; leadership varies too much by individual and situational circumstances to build a theory around personal characteristics alone (this is not to say, however, that they are unimportant because their possession is necessary for leadership).

Traits include: (a) physical features, (b) personality attributes, (c) motivational characteristics, (d) value dispositions, and (e) general aptitudes. Many would like to think that physical features should not bear on leadership, but comportment does: a leader's physical presence may give followers a sense of assurance and well-being. Personality attributes (self-confidence, decisiveness, resilience, flexibility, energy, and willingness to assume responsibility) are powerfully correlated with leadership. Yet despite their importance, no traits are absolute. Further, they may be vitiated. Self-confidence, for instance, encourages followers (even if the leader has a poor idea), but excessive confidence can degrade into egotism, stubbornness, or aloofness.

Just as significant are motivational traits (McClelland 1985). Perhaps the most vital is the need to achieve. Institutions produce goods and services; those individuals with achievement needs project them through organizational accomplishments. They also share certain value dispositions that have a special cast in public service. Nearly every study of followers' preferences puts leader honesty-integrity-fairness at the top of the list. Because of the stewardship role, these values have a nearly hallowed stature that when absent tarnishes reputations (Fairholm 1991; Terry 1995; Riccucci 1995). Another value is the drive for excellence. Additional values, which may be more desirable in the government and non-profit sectors than in business, include a public service motivation and cultural sensitivity. The final set of traits is generalized aptitude. Although there are many worthy candidates (e.g., intelligence and creativity), most researchers identify emotional maturity as essential because it allows people to balance interests, to be resilient, and to see "the big picture."

It is difficult to sharply demarcate traits, which are innate, early-imprinted characteristics, from skills, which are more susceptible to change with learning, especially in adulthood. While leaders need technical skills—technical credibility or expertise can be an important source of power (French and Raven 1959)—the amount and type usually shifts according to the level in an organization. A second area is interpersonal skills and communication skills. They become increasingly important when moving from supervisory to middle management to executive positions (Katz 1955). Communication skills encompass the use of verbal, oral, and written media, as well as nonverbal communication.

Influencing and negotiating skills rely on both specific interaction competencies and the wise use of power. Power in administrative settings provides a dichotomy: It stems partially from the position as well as from its occupant. In the extreme cases, some people wield power entirely through position (and generally without much popularity) and, though less common, some people wield considerable power lacking a formal position. The final skill is continual learning. Although it has become a popular concept and

Table 4.2

Key Traits and Skills

Leader characteristics

Traits
  1. Physical traits:
     • *Comportment:* Does the leader carry her/himself in a way that earns respect?

  2. Personal traits (stable personality dispositions):
     • *Self-confidence:* Does he or she have an appropriate "can-do" attitude?
     • *Decisiveness:* Does the person make relatively rapid decisions when these are pressing or straightforward decisions, but more deliberative and inclusive decisions at other times?
     • *Resilience:* Does the individual avoid letting discouragement of failures, setbacks, or even hard work affect their attitude or interactions with subordinates?
     • *Flexibility:* Does the leader have the ability to adapt plans that are not working well? Can the leader size up alternatives for important work initiatives?
     • *Energy:* Does he or she have enough physical and mental energy to keep many projects going simultaneously as well as motivate other people?
     • *Willingness to assume responsibility:* Is the leader willing to assume responsibility for what goes wrong as well as what goes right? Is the leader willing to take on extra assignments for the good of the organization?

  3. Motivational traits (desire for stimulus):
     • *Need for achievement:* Does the leader have a strong need for achievement? Is this need balanced by a strong awareness of others' need for recognition and achievement as well?

  4. Value traits:
     • *Fairness/integrity/honesty:* Is there a strongly honed sense of fairness, integrity, and honesty?
     • *Drive for excellence:* Does the leader try to achieve more than just past performance, the average, or minimum expectations in as many areas as possible?
     • *Service motivation and customer service orientation:* Is there a strong sense of the importance of ensuring that clients/citizens/customers have the best service? Does the leader ensure that they have ample opportunities to be heard?

  5. Aptitudes (inherent generalized capacities):
     • *Emotional maturity:* Does the leader have the ability to put everything into perspective? Is the leader able to keep personal needs and crises from adversely affecting work performance?
Skills
  1. *Technical skills (technical credibility):* Does the leader have the technical skills to adequately monitor and assess the jobs of subordinates?

(continued)

2. *Communication:* Is the leader's verbal communication clear, motivating, and even inspiring? Is written communication clear, timely, thorough, and even inspiring at times?

3. *Influencing and negotiating/power:* Does the leader use a variety of influencing skills rather than just position power?

4. *Continual learning:* Does the leader demonstrate ability to continually learn new ideas? Does he or she learn from subordinates and outside experts?

---

has been democratized to cover much of the workforce, it has long been recognized as an important executive/leadership skill. Table 4.2 summarizes those characteristics found to be important in the literature, and the inventory in Exhibit 4.2 measures one's leadership traits. These traits are found in action as the S&L case continues.

Leader Characteristics and the Savings and Loan Debacle

Because so many powerful people had an interest in covering up the crisis, it took more than an assessment of the problem as noted in the initial installment; it required standing up to prominent people again and again. When the White House refused to add regulators, Black recommended to the chair of the FHLBB that he privatize bank examiners by having them transferred to the twelve Federal Home Loan district banks across the country. Chairman Gray then instructed the banks to double their examiner staffs. When House Speaker Jim Wright (D-TX) intervened more and more aggressively on behalf of Texas thrifts, and verbally attacked Black in person, Black responded by publicly divulging the politically motivated obstruction actions. Wright was removed as Speaker based on this and other ethics charges and resigned from his seat in 1989.

When Senators Riegle, DeConcini, McCain, Cranston, and Glenn (the Keating Five) summoned Black to a private meeting and tried to get him to ease up on Lincoln Savings and Loan, he turned the tables on them: He filed criminal charges against the thrift because it was considered the most corrupt in America. The

Exhibit 4.2

Leadership Trait Questionnaire

Instructions: The purpose of this questionnaire is to measure personal characteristics of leadership. The questionnaire should be completed by the leader and five individuals who are familiar with the leader.

For each adjective listed below, indicate the degree to which you think the adjective describes the leader. Please select one of the following responses to indicate the strength of your opinion.

Key: 5 = Strongly agree 4 = Agree 3 = Neutral 2 = Disagree 1 = Strongly disagree

1. Articulate–Communicates effectively
    with others.   1 2 3 4 5

2. Perceptive–Discerning and insightful.   1 2 3 4 5

3. Self-confident–Believes in oneself and
   one's ability.   1 2 3 4 5

4. Self-assured–Secure with self, free of
   doubts   1 2 3 4 5

5. Persistent–Stays fixed on the goal(s),
   despite interference.   1 2 3 4 5

6. Determined–Takes a firm stand, acts
   with certainty.   1 2 3 4 5

7. Trustworthy–Acts believable, inspires
   confidence.   1 2 3 4 5

8. Dependable–Is consistent and reliable.   1 2 3 4 5

9. Friendly–Shows kindness and warmth.   1 2 3 4 5

10. Outgoing–Talks freely, gets along well
    with others.   1 2 3 4 5

Scoring Interpretation

The scores you received on the LTQ provide information about how you see yourself and how others see you as a leader. The

(continued)

Exhibit 4.2 *(continued)*

chart allows you to see where your perceptions are the same as others and where they differ from others.

There are no best ratings on this questionnaire. The purpose of the instrument is to give you a way to assess your strengths and weaknesses and to evaluate areas where your perceptions are congruent with others and where there are discrepancies.

Source: Northouse (2003: 31). Copyright © 2003 Sage Publications, Inc. Reprinted with permission.

---

owner, Charles Keating, was ultimately sentenced to ten years in prison without parole. The cost to taxpayers from that single institution was 2.5 billion dollars. Board member Lee Henkel (who had worked for Keating), proposed regulations that would have exempted his former boss's institution. Black exposed the scheme and Henkel was forced to resign and later was prohibited from working in the field altogether. When Gray's term expired, his replacement, Danny Wall (a one-time thrift owner) tried to block Black at every turn. Black refused to capitulate or be pushed out and blew the whistle on him and some of the most important people in the nation.

In trying to bring the scandal under control, Black's leader characteristics become evident. He had to:

- be self-confident and comport himself well even when personally attacked by elected officials;
- be decisive in finding unique strategies to use in takeovers or mergers of scores of insolvent S&Ls;
- respond with resilience and flexibility when corrupt bankers or politicians tried to outmaneuver him;
- have high amounts of energy to prosecute cases while highlighting the seriousness of the problems and the liability to the public;

- be willing to take on this challenge for modest pay out of a sense of dedication and achievement;
- retain unimpeachable integrity;
- set high standards of performance and excellence for his examiners in the cause of the public's good (i.e., service motivation); and
- remain calm under pressure from major politicians, as well as from the years of political in-fighting (i.e., exhibit emotional maturity).

Black had the right skills for the job. He had the economics and legal training required in order to disentangle complex financial dealings and to be able to prosecute illegal ones. He was verbally gifted so that he was able to convince those not already committed to reform. He was willing or able to use a wide range of influence and negotiation tactics from rational persuasion to personal pleas. Finally, as the problems evolved—and grew— he knew he had to continually learn new ways to approach the crisis he worked to contain. All of these traits and skills would need to come together into a coherent style appropriate for the situation (discussed in the next section).

Leadership Styles

Style, the third aspect (Exhibit 4.3), refers to dominant and defining behavioral patterns. One can speak of a single, overall style, but few leaders have one approach that they use all the time; styles vary from situation to situation. Leaders may use styles consciously but as often as not they do so unconsciously and may even be oblivious that some of their actions belie their espoused style (the one they say they have). Followers also attribute styles to leaders from the behaviors they observe; these may or may not be consistent because of different observations and perspectives about the leader. Successful executives know what modes are needed in given situations, what their styles are, and consciously adapt their approach or the situation (or both) for maximum success (Hersey and Blanchard 1969; Fiedler, Chemers, and Mahar 1976). The style questions in Exhibit 4.3 measure types of behaviors: task and relationship.

Many factors impinge upon styles: follower characteristics, environmental contingencies, and power structures. A leader would not use the same style with new recruits as with twenty-five-year veteran employees. Nor would one use the same tact with someone about to be suspended as one would use with an award-winning employee. The most prominent environmental contingency is a crisis in which directive modes and sheer decisiveness are at a premium. The culture of the organization or unit also will impact the style chosen. It is common in large divisions or agencies, where there are substantial external contacts to maintain, for the CEO to focus on external affairs and the chief deputy to handle internal operations, resulting in a dual leadership model affecting the styles that the respective individuals employ.

Leader qualities also include preferred/secondary styles, style range, style capacity, and orientations toward change. People have preferred and secondary leadership styles. The preferred is the one that a person feels most comfortable with and relies upon in ambiguous situations; secondary styles are those that can be employed, but generally in a more self-conscious manner. Style range is the degree to which the leader can use multiple approaches. Style capacity is the ability to apply a style effectively. It is quite possible that one official would have great capacity only in one style, and rarely utilize others, and for another to have a comprehensive range and wield all poorly. Effective leaders not only have competence in a wide style range, but are able to shift styles. There is controversy about how much a given individual can change style or adapt to circumstances (Fiedler, Chemers, and Mahar 1976). Yet even adopting a narrow view of adaptability, he or she is responsible for either adapting situations in amenable ways or finding the right person to handle them.

Are leaders primarily maintainers of systems or facilitators of change? Management activities are called "transactional" and the change activities are called "transformational" in scope (Zalenik

Exhibit 4.3

Style Questionnaire

Instructions: Read each item carefully and think about how often you (or the person you are evaluating) engage in the described behavior. Indicate your response to each item by circling one of the five numbers to the right of each item.

Key: 1 = Never 2 = Seldom 3 = Occasionally 4 = Often 5 = Always

1. Tells group members what they are supposed to do.   1 2 3 4 5
2. Acts friendly with members of the group.   1 2 3 4 5
3. Sets standards of performance for group members.   1 2 3 4 5
4. Helps others feel comfortable in the group.   1 2 3 4 5
5. Makes suggestions about how to solve problems.   1 2 3 4 5
6. Responds favorably to suggestions made by others.   1 2 3 4 5
7. Makes his or her perspective clear to others.   1 2 3 4 5
8. Treats others fairly.   1 2 3 4 5
9. Develops a plan of action for the group.   1 2 3 4 5
10. Behaves in a predictable manner toward group members.   1 2 3 4 5
11. Defines role responsibilities for each group member.   1 2 3 4 5
12. Communicates actively with group members.   1 2 3 4 5
13. Clarifies his or her own role within the group.   1 2 3 4 5
14. Shows concern for the personal well-being of others.   1 2 3 4 5
15. Provides a plan for how the work is to be done.   1 2 3 4 5
16. Shows flexibility in making decisions.   1 2 3 4 5
17. Provides criteria for what is expected of the group.   1 2 3 4 5

(continued)

Exhibit 4.3 *(continued)*

18. Discloses thoughts and feelings to group
    members.   1 2 3 4 5
19. Encourages group members to do quality
    work.   1 2 3 4 5
20. Helps group members get along.   1 2 3 4 5

Scoring

The style questionnaire is designed to measure two major types of leadership behaviors: task and relationship. Score the questionnaire by doing the following. First, sum the responses on the odd-numbered items. This is your task score. Second, sum the responses on the even-numbered items. This is your relationship score.

Total scores: Task _____   Relationship _____

Scoring Interpretation

45–50   Very high range
40–44   High range
35–39   Moderately high range
30–34   Moderately low range
25–29   Low range
10–24   Very low range

Source: Northouse (2003: 82). Copyright © 2003 Sage Publications, Inc. Reprinted with permission.

1977). Each category can be further divided into leadership with a task, people, or organizational focus. Thus transformational styles can include entrepreneurial (task), charismatic (people), or organizational (visionary) emphases. A variety of styles are demonstrated by Black in his quest to clean up the S&L industry.

The Savings and Loan Scandal and Leader Styles

Black's role in dealing with S&Ls is an excellent example of leadership growth. When initially hired under Gray, he focused on technical and personnel issues. As a task-oriented manager, he took overt action in the litigation of cases, planned who would pursue them, and kept staff informed. As an entrepreneurial leader, he solved technical legal problems and found new ways to overcome political hurdles. As a people-oriented manager, he regularly consulted with bank examiners, trained new examiners, developed their skills in handling complex cases, and kept them motivated when setbacks occurred. As a charismatic leader, he provided a strong sense of team spirit for the embattled examiners, acted as an inspiring role model, and convinced others outside the organization of the seriousness of the problem. While Gray was the chair of the FHLBB, Black frequently made recommendations about organization-level strategy, but he did not need to be in charge.

That all changed when Danny Wall became the chair in 1987. His aim was to get Black fired. (Black had moved to a regional bank and thus was technically not a government employee— but he functioned in the same capacity as the head of bank examiners.) Wall also wanted to downplay the crisis until after the 1988 presidential election. Even from a much-weakened position, Black became engaged as an organizational leader. He made public accusations against Speaker Wright, the five senators, and prosecuted high-visibility cases. While powerful players were able to outflank him temporarily (such as when Wall moved jurisdiction for the Keating S&L away from Black's region so that he could delay its closing), Black ultimately was able to maintain public pressure. He was able to be successful as a leader only because he adapted his style to various situations, and increased his competence in those different styles.

Had Black not been successful it is possible that the scandal would have cost twice as much; it could have been blamed largely on banking conditions (e.g., high interest rates) rather than on corruption and fraud; and Black could have been outmaneuvered permanently, could have become discouraged and quit, or could have been fired. None of these things happened because, in summary, he had the technical competence to pursue cases successfully, despite interference from Congress. He also had the ethical fortitude to persevere in the public interest at the risk of his own career. And he had the leadership ability to assess the situation, draw on his personal skills (e.g., such as oratorical eloquence), and change his leadership style to suit the challenges he faced.

Leader Behaviors

Although traits and skills supply the reservoir of talent, and styles provide approaches to the leadership, it is through behaviors that goals are fulfilled. Behaviors can be divided into task, people, and organizational activities. Task-oriented behaviors (monitoring, planning operations, clarifying roles, informing, delegating, problem solving, and carrying out frontline innovation are types of technical competencies.

While professionals require task expertise, to be leaders they need people and organizational skills too. People-oriented talents include consulting, personnel planning, employee motivation, team building, as well as conflict and change management. Because leaders work through others, such abilities are indispensable. Professionals also need strong organizational competencies: environmental scanning, strategic planning, vision articulation, networking, decision-making, and managing organizational change (Table 4.3).

Exhibit 4.4 (on pp. 108–9) measures the reader's technical, human, and conceptual leadership behaviors and skills. The discussion of Black's experiences has alluded to a number of key competencies:

• His assessment skills (e.g., the behavioral competencies of monitoring, consulting, and scanning the environment) of his own organization and the external environment were acute. He had to accurately gauge his examiners' skills, identify evolving problems in numerous separate investigations, and constantly scan the political environment for impending assaults on his examiner teams.

• His technical and task ability to audit and prosecute so many

Table 4.3

Leader Behaviors and Style Domains

	Task	People	Organizational
Assessment and evaluation	1. Monitor and assess tasks	1. Consult	1. Scan the environment
Formulation and planning functions	2. Plan operations	2. Plan and organize personnel	2. Do strategic planning
Implementation functions	3. Clarify roles and objectives	3. Develop staff	3. Network and partner
	4. Inform	4. Motivate	4. Perform general management functions
	5. Delegate	5. Build and manage teams	5. Articulate the mission and vision
Change functions	6. Solve problems	6. Manage conflict	6. Make decisions
	7. Manage innovation and creativity	7. Manage personal change	7. Manage organizational change

cases demonstrated he was able to set up systems in which everyone knew who was doing what and in which there was a great deal of delegated power (e.g., the behavioral competencies of operations planning, role clarification, informing, delegating, problem solving, and managing technical innovation). One of Black's great strengths was that he had extensive financial and legal training. Further, he had the knack of hiring competent people, clarifying their roles, and getting out of their way until and unless political overtones emerged.

• His mastery at building effective audit teams enabled his highly motivated staff to tackle new types of fraud (e.g., the behavioral competencies of personnel planning, motivating, building teams, managing conflict, and managing personal change). Black had to be able to organize project teams that had the necessary set of complementary skills (Katzenbach and Smith 1993), stayed motivated despite heavy workloads and setbacks, worked cooperatively, and resisted internal conflict. He has had to help them rapidly adapt their investigative and litigating practices as the enormity of the scandal evolved.

• His ability for working at the "systems" level and his talent in creating a compelling vision were remarkable (e.g., the behavioral competencies of strategic planning, networking, general management functions, mission articulation, decision making, and managing organizational change). No matter what his position was—deputy director of a federal agency or head of an examiner division in a private bank—Black was able to work with people from many areas, integrate strategies, and provide a convincing ideal for rectifying a national travesty.

Leader Evaluation of Organization and Self

Leader evaluation is the end of one cycle, but it is the basis for much of the next. It should occur at regular intervals, but ultimately it is an ongoing activity too. First and foremost, leaders will be examining the appropriate balance among the institution's technical performance, follower development, and organizational alignment. Which areas need primary focus in the upcoming period?

Exhibit 4.4

Skills Inventory

Instructions: Read each item carefully and decide whether the item describes you as a person. Indicate your response to each item by circling one of the five numbers to the right of each item.

Key: 1 = Not true 2 = Seldom true 3 = Occasionally true 4 = Somewhat true 5 = Very true

1. I enjoy getting into the details of how things work. 1 2 3 4 5
2. As a rule, adapting ideas to people's needs is relatively easy for me. 1 2 3 4 5
3. I enjoy working with abstract ideas. 1 2 3 4 5
4. Technical things fascinate me. 1 2 3 4 5
5. Being able to understand others is the most important part of my work. 1 2 3 4 5
6. Seeing the "big picture" comes easy for me. 1 2 3 4 5
7. One of my skills is being good at making things work. 1 2 3 4 5
8. My main concern is to have a supportive communication climate. 1 2 3 4 5
9. I am intrigued by complex organizational problems. 1 2 3 4 5
10. Following directions and filling out forms comes easily for me. 1 2 3 4 5
11. Understanding the social fabric of the organization is important to me. 1 2 3 4 5
12. I would enjoy working out strategies for my organization's growth. 1 2 3 4 5
13. I am good at completing the things I've been assigned to do. 1 2 3 4 5
14. Getting all parties to work together is a challenge I enjoy. 1 2 3 4 5
15. Creating a mission statement is rewarding work. 1 2 3 4 5

(continued)

Exhibit 4.4 *(continued)*

16. I understand how to do the basic things
    required of me.   1 2 3 4 5
17. I am concerned with how my decisions
    affect the lives of others.   1 2 3 4 5
18. Thinking about organizational values and
    philosophy appeals to me.   1 2 3 4 5

Scoring

The skills inventory is designed to measure three broad types of leadership skills: technical, human, and conceptual. Score the questionnaire by doing the following. First, sum the responses on items 1, 4, 7, 10, 13, and 16. This is your technical skill score. Second, sum the responses on items 2, 5, 8, 11, 14, and 17. This is your human skill score. Third, sum the responses on items 3, 6, 9, 12, 15, and 18. This is your conceptual skill score.

Total scores: Technical skill _____   Human skill _____
Conceptual skill _____

Scoring Interpretation

The scores you received on the skills inventory provide information about your leadership skills in three areas. By comparing the differences between your scores you can determine where you have leadership strengths and where you have leadership weaknesses. Your scores also point toward the level of management for which you might be most suited.

In terms of change focus, leaders will analyze the success of past strategic initiatives and the concrete change management that accompanied them. Is the overall strategy sound? Is the change implementation at an operational level working? Leaders will also look at the more operational aspects of processes to see if quality improvements are necessary. Finally, they need to look at the evolutionary stages of organizational need and how this fits with the environment, strategy, and operations.

Last but certainly not least, professionals must look at themselves and their roles. Do they need to redeploy their own energies based on their evaluation? Should they change their style in particular situations or perhaps in general to meet evolving conditions? And are they continuing to develop themselves, to accommodate the changing needs of the institution and the need to continually learn for their own self-development and renewal? Exhibit 4.5 shows the devastating consequences of leadership failure in at least one part of a Midwest state.

A Leader's Continuing Evaluation and an Industry Epilogue

Black had to continually reevaluate the health of the S&L industry, and his ability to do the most good for it. The largest decision occurred in 1987, when he left the deputy director position at the FSLIC, and became and the head of examiners of a region (technically not a federal position). This was a difficult decision because Black liked to be a direct combatant in the fight to restore the soundness of the thrift industry. However, he had done what he could do as an insider, and he evaluated that he could do more good as an outsider. From his new position, he (along with a growing chorus of concerned voices) was able to apply a great deal of pressure on Congress to handle the escalating crisis in a comprehensive way.

After the 1988 election, Congress passed the 1989 Financial Institution Reform, Recovery, and Enforcement Act. Because of a lack of confidence in the existing structures with the loss of personnel, Congress abolished both the FHLBB and the FSLIC. It

Exhibit 4.5

Is the United Way the Only Way?

Mike Schuler, *Quid Est Disputatum* Consulting

Thousands of individuals who depend on the United Way of America—and the many organizations that donate money and time for food, clothing, shelter, prescriptions, and emergency services—have been victimized. "Most of the criticism is aimed at the Washington, D.C., area's office, where the local United Way was found to have misused federal employee donations. In other cities, time put in by unpaid volunteers had been assigned a dollar value and counted as a cash contribution" (Weber 2002). For example, public donations may never look the same for the Capital Area United Way (CAUW) in East Lansing, Michigan, as the result of a recent scandal.

Imprisoned former finance chief of the agency, Jacquelyn Allen-MacGregor, devised an elaborate check-writing scheme to accumulate $1.88 million spent on horses and property in Texas. Just a year after, United Way President Bill Aramony was convicted on 25 counts of stealing from the national organization. Such incidents suggest a larger problem for the United Way and perhaps other nonprofit organizations. Indeed, as a participant in the 2003 Council of Foundations convention asked, "Why is our world looking like Worldcom and Enron?" (Labbe 2003).

The CAUW CEO resigned calling the embezzlement "my worst nightmare." "The Board of Directors and I take our stewardship responsibilities to our donors very seriously. We feel betrayed in the extreme by a long-time, trusted employee" (Reynaert 2002). "It is worth noting," former chair of the CAUW Board, Patrick Scheetz, said, "that the controls circumvented by the embezzler were considered by financial experts to be significantly more extensive than those in use at many large, nonprofit organizations" (Reynaert 2002). The Board reaffirmed its objectives: (1) restitution/recovery of the embezzled funds, (2) prosecution of the person or persons responsible, and (3) making sure that nothing like this can ever happen again." Nonetheless, if a criminal

(continued)

Exhibit 4.5 *(continued)*

could work over seven years in an institution with "significantly more extensive" accounting measures, then what is to say this "can never happen again?"

Many in the community wonder about the "myth" of the United Way as an indispensable agency. The CAUW, which serves a tri-county area and raises between five and ten million annually, has in-depth knowledge of the community and provides important services for those less fortunate in mid-Michigan (Liles 2003). Yet, it was not just one alleged criminal who allowed scandal to happen; it was a systemic failure by the organization to prevent the losses (Melot 2003b), and symptomatic of a larger problem directed at trusting nonprofit agencies. Some communities are embracing an alternative to administrative-heavy organizations like the United Way, which earmarks 13 percent of giving for operating costs. For instance, America's Charities (www.charities.org) and CreateHope (www.createhope.com) facilitate community development through electronic donations—for half the cost of what United Way charges for administering a fund-raising campaign. "They're putting a fresh face on charity" (Melot 2003a) by dispelling the myth that the United Way is the "only way" to foster community development.

However, the United Way is resistant to such changes and continues to rely on its traditional fund-raising campaign technique. Recently, CAUW's new chairman of the board, Tom Chirgwin, attempted to rebuild the trust of donors by announcing a new slogan for the nonprofit. "A new day, a new way." In his "state of the United Way" address during a public Q&A session where 250 community members assembled, Chirgwin outlined five strategies:

- clearer, more focused oversight of the operations, specifically related to finances;
- promises to revamp the board of directors, which potentially means better representation for segments of the community that have had little voice on the board;

(continued)

Exhibit 4.5 *(continued)*

- consulting with, and listening to, the concerns of United Way agencies by asking for suggestions on improving services;
- a code of conduct for the charity's staff and board members; and
- a donor bill of rights, which, among other things, will allow donors to review United Way's financial records (Melot 2003b).

The results of these strategies are yet to be seen. The organization feels it has taken appropriate and preemptive measures in outlining this strategy. For the sake of the community, its donors, and 120,000 service recipients, it is hoped that the measures taken do not rest with a slogan alone, but instead facilitate a needed transformation.

---

completely reconstituted the system with the Office of Thrift Supervision (an agency under the Treasury Department) for enforcement, the Savings Association Insurance Fund (under the Federal Deposit Insurance Corporation), and the independent Resolution Trust Corporation (RTC) to sell off the enormous backlog of assets that the government acquired due to the torrent of S&L failures. When it did so, it refinanced the system and gave it new enforcement powers to clean up the mess. In the 1989–95 period when the RTC and its sister institutions restored order and integrity in the industry, more than 750 thrift institutions were closed or merged by the federal government and many more merged on their own accord to liquidate dwindling resources. In addition, thousands of S&L owners were prosecuted for repayment and criminal activity. In fact, 3,700 senior executives and owners of failed thrifts actually served time in prison. By 1995 when the RTC closed its doors (it was created as a temporary agency), the worst of the crisis was over, and the industry was back in good health with sound practices (DiConti 1998).

Summary and Conclusion

This chapter provided a snapshot of leadership based on research and observations about what effective leaders must be aware of. It should be quickly apparent that leadership is complex and difficult in the best of circumstances. The extensive case study not only illustrates the complexity and difficulty of public service leadership, but the requirement for technical and ethical competencies discussed in chapters two and three. Black was the man who did more to clean up the quarter-trillion-dollar S&L mess than any other single individual (Riccucci 1995). He often had to work at odds with the most powerful men in America. Despite this extraordinary feat, this hero—who served the populace in both public and private employment—is almost unknown and unacknowledged. Fortunately, he came to his job with exceptional technical competence in legal and financial areas. Further, he was endowed with a high level of moral clarity and courage that he was able to draw upon as he struggled to fix a problem that other leaders wanted to bequeath to the future.

Yet even technical expertise and ethical wisdom and perseverance are not enough for one to be a great leader. Professionals must be able to astutely assess their organization, the environment, and the constraints that they face. Based on the assessment, they should be able to set realistic but challenging goals to achieve their agency's mission, mitigate organizational weaknesses, and build on institutional strengths. They must come with a variety of traits and skills such as self-confidence, energy, a drive for excellence, a capacity to communicate effectively, an ability to use power wisely, and a propensity to learn continuously. They must be able to amalgamate their traits and skills into an appropriate style based on the needs of differing situations. Because of the awesome array of responsibilities, professionals should be proficient in task-oriented, people-oriented, and organizational-oriented behavioral competencies. As leaders observe the performance of organizations under their tutelage, they must be able to objectively evaluate these accomplishments. This triggers the next phase of leadership as the initial assessment phase begins anew.

Black, the administrative exemplar of the professional edge, demonstrated all these elements. His methodical assessment of his organization meant that it was always elevated to its highest level of performance. Even more impressive was the assessment of legal limitations, political interventions, and resource constraints that he faced. Rather than being daunted by the enormity of the constraints, he worked to alleviate them by moving his job to the private sector (to mitigate legal restrictions), using the media (to discourage political interference), and learning ways of doing more with less (to get the job done). Second, he had a full complement of the important traits and skills, from optimism to open-mindedness. Third, time and again, he adapted his style, from the quiet analytic style of an audit examiner, to the eloquent legal style of a prosecutor, and even to the feisty style of a political operative. Fourth, although not specifically trained in management and leadership, Black learned all of the many behavioral competencies that are required to do it well. For example, he had to be an operations planner, a team motivator, and a visionary able to enthuse all with whom he came in contact. Finally, he had to be able to judge his failures and setbacks as objectively as successes and victories, in order to evolve with his organization and the political-financial environment.

Public service professionals—from program supervisor to chief executive officer—take challenges seriously. On one hand, they learn to practice the art of leadership (DePree 1989). That is, they use their intuition, passion, and personal uniqueness to create purpose and public value. Leaders such as Black are able to draw on their inner strengths and beliefs as they pursue the common good. On the other hand, they also practice the hardnosed science of leadership as a series of processes and skills that must be mastered through disciplined study and reflective experience. Passion or goodwill do little good without an organized approach to leadership. If Black had been a poor planner, weak at team building, or unable to articulate a captivating mission, he would have been unsuccessful. Yet although his example may be dramatic, many professionals perform effectively and conscientiously every day for the benefit of the people they both lead and serve, as will be shown in the final chapter.

— Chapter 5 —

The Future of Public Service
Cases and Commentary for the New Millennium

Only they deserve power who justify its use daily.
—Dag Hammarskjöld

The consummate professional integrates the technical, ethical, and leadership dimensions of her craft. The result is the professional edge: It is unthinkable not to do one's best. One knows the work by the workman; no one is in a hurry for the wrong answer. Today, public service professionals find their responsibilities affected by a host of trends and issues: downsizing, homeland security, contracting reforms, an aging staff, performance measurements, citizen demands, and the thinning of management ranks already eroded by a decade of cutbacks. Accordingly, they must excel at old skills and develop new ones by focusing on:

- Technical acumen (e.g., financial, human, information resources)
- Ethical results (accountability, credibility, integrity)
- Leading change (vision, strategy, coalition building and conflict resolution, resilience, flexibility, service to the public; adapted from National Academy of Public Administration 2003).

As public servants learn more about governance in the information age, it is understood that success depends upon human capital.

Professionals confront this question: "Do they have sufficient ability in the triangle of competencies to meet the challenges they confront?" For example, is the technical expertise present to manage the installation of a cutting-edge information system, the ethical ability to make complicated human resource decisions, or the leadership capacity to motivate people? Professionals rarely have the luxury of being merely technical experts, avoiding ethical decisions, or shunning leadership roles. Instead they must be able to move seamlessly from one point of the triangle to another in performing public service.

In so doing, they must to be able to weigh competing needs: personal (seeking advancement and fulfillment), professional (achieving standards), organizational (driving for program effectiveness), legal needs (adhering to administrative rules), and public interest (protecting the commonweal; Van Wart 1998). Professionals, by definition, are adept at detecting the underlying value issues, balancing them in an appropriate manner to fit the unique characteristics of each situation, and explaining the rationale in decision making. When one set of needs is overemphasized at the expense of another, problems occur. Some examples:

- the architect who designs a building without consulting with the users (technical arrogance);
- the auditor who excoriates a small nonprofit for minor fiscal and process problems while neglecting to note accomplishment (technical formalism);
- the business executive who suppresses a scandal (ethical pathology);
- the manager who hires an adequate but less qualified friend (nepotism); and
- the government agency, not-for-profit, or commercial vendor who efficiently carries out a mandated policy, but fails to tell policymakers that it is not a good value for the money (leadership failure).

The democratic context of public service requires a healthy and open debate about competing values to avoid issues like these.

The failure to do so is illustrated by a recent probe into the Nature Conservancy (Exhibit 5.1); based on that report, the United States Senate launched its own investigation into the charity's accounting practices and real estate deals in late 2003.

To highlight the need for complementary competencies and to illustrate public service challenges, three case studies are discussed. These are then capped by an examination of the first pervasive challenge in the new millennium—the Enron Era—as a way to understand the present and to peer into the future.

Episodes in Public Service

Melding technical, ethical, and leadership aspects of professionalism is shown in cases involving cyberwarfare, fire suppression, and trash collection.

Cyberwarfare

A new policy that envisions an entirely new type of warfare, one that substitutes—or supplements—bombs and troops with cyberweapons is under development (episode excerpted from Graham 2003; also refer to Berkowitz 2003; Ziegler 2003; Brzezinski 2003).

> President George Bush has signed a secret directive ordering the government, for the first time, national-level guidance for determining when and how the United States would launch cyberattacks against enemy computer networks. Similar to strategic doctrine that has guided the use of nuclear weapons since World War II, the cyberwarfare guidance would establish the rules under which foreign computer systems would be penetrated and disrupted.
>
> The United States has never conducted a large-scale, strategic cyberattack. But the Pentagon has stepped up development of cyberweapons, envisioning a day when electrons might substitute for bombs and allow for more rapid and less bloody attacks on enemy targets. Instead of risking planes or troops, military planners imagine soldiers at computer terminals silently invading foreign networks to shut down radars, disable electrical facilities, and disrupt phone services.

Exhibit 5.1

The Nature Conservancy

The Nature Conservancy has blossomed into the world's richest environmental group, amassing $3 billion in assets by pledging to save precious places. Known for its advertisements decorated with forest, streams and the soothing voice of actor Paul Newman, the 52-year-old charity preserves millions of acres across the nation. Yet the Conservancy has logged forests, engineered a $64 million deal paving the way for opulent houses on fragile grasslands and drilled for natural gas under the last breeding ground of an endangered bird species.

Based in Arlington, Va., its governing board and advisory council now includes executives and directors from oil companies, chemical producers, auto manufacturers, mining concerns, logging operations, and coal-burning electric utilities. Some of those corporations have paid millions in environmental fines. It is the leading proponent of a brand of environmentalism that promotes compromise between conservation and corporate America.

The Conservancy defends its partnership with loggers by arguing that it has persuaded them to adopt more conservation-friendly methods. The Dogwood Alliance, a coalition of 70 grassroots environmental groups, says the change in methods is superficial and the damage remains considerable. Further the partnership gives loggers a public relations boost from "greenwashing" [corporate environmental propaganda—authors' note] Dogwood and other environmental groups charge.

A January 15, 2003, internal Conservancy memo worried that the charity would be portrayed as if it had "systematically colluded with wealthy individuals and corporations to conduct land transactions that manipulate the tax code to the benefit of the affluent." Conservancy executives feared that their organization might be depicted as an "environmental Enron."

_____

Source: Condensed from Ottaway and Stephens (2003).

Bush's action highlights the administration's keen interest in pursuing a new form of weaponry that many specialists say has great potential for altering the means of waging war, but that until now has lacked presidential rules for deciding the circumstances under which such attacks would be launched, who should authorize and conduct them, and what targets would be considered legitimate.

Despite months of discussions involving principally the Pentagon, CIA, FBI, and National Security Agency, officials say a number of issues remain far from resolved. The current state of planning has been likened to the early years following the invention of the atomic bomb more than a half-century ago, when thinking about how to wage nuclear war lagged the ability to launch one.

In a move to consult with experts outside government, White House officials helped arrange a meeting at the Massachusetts Institute of Technology that attracted about fifty participants. But a number expressed reservations about engaging in cyberattacks, arguing that the United States' own enormous dependence on computer networks makes it highly vulnerable to counterattack. (Graham 2003: 29–30)

To summarize, cyberwarfare technical skill appears available, ethical competency can be applied as war-fighting scenarios are created, and leadership ability may develop as experience is gained in war games. A careful assessment of all three points of the professional triangle clearly will be needed in the years ahead as for-profit contractors increasingly are involved in national defense functions (Wayne 2002).

Forest Service Fire Suppression, Then and Now

In the next case, the U.S. Forest Service has always had a conflicting, multiuse philosophy including support of commercial cutting, forest sustainability, wildlife protection, and recreation (Dubnick 1998). The importance of the competing interests means that the competency triangle must be fully engaged to create policy in an often highly turbulent environment (Kaufman 1960; O'Neill and Christopher 2002).

One dramatic challenge that the Forest Service had to confront near the end of the twentieth century was its controversial fire suppression policy (*National Fire Plan Implementation* 2001). The implicit policy that had been practiced was that any-and-all fire was bad and should be suppressed wherever and whenever possible (Smokey the Bear's famous motto: "Only you can prevent forest fires" symbolizes the approach). Yet as it turns out, the very success of fire suppression since the 1930s left most forests more vulnerable to catastrophic, rather than regenerative, fires. Fires occur in nature because of lightning and dryness under normal conditions, and periodically "clean" forests of ground debris and excessive young growth (crowding). In the 1930s, up to 40 million acres of land burned every year; that had been reduced to less than 5 million acres by the beginning of the 1990s. Most earlier fires would consume excess fuel on forest floors, burn much of the younger growth (allowing larger, older trees to survive in a healthier environment), and were seen as regenerative or "cool" fires.

By the late 1980s, it was clear that the suppression policy was not working well. Fires were increasingly frequent, dangerous, and uncontainable as almost all were catastrophic or "hot" fires. They not only burned the largest trees, but the enormous amount of accumulated debris on forest floors caused the soil itself to be burned down to eighteen inches deep. Thus nature's tremendous regenerative powers were generally eliminated. Furthermore, fires moved faster and survival became less likely for people or animals in their paths.

Suppression policies were unsustainable in the long run because of accumulated effects of an *absence* of periodic fires. To respond to the emergent crisis, the Forest Service proposed a new management style in 1996 (Reuters 1996). Joined by the Department of the Interior, the agencies supported a new National Fire Plan that was authorized in 2000. Forest service professionals promoted two policies. First, the agency was adding a tool called a "prescribed burn" to its arsenal. Such burns allow it to start controlled fires in areas that have been physically prepared and have fire personnel ready for control purposes. Unfortunately, in 2000 near Los Alamos, New Mexico, a prescribed burn that "escaped" and destroyed many homes brought the policy under intense criticism. The second policy was renewed forest thinning, allowing the cutting of all trees under twelve inches in diameter by commercial interests. The distrust of the environmentalists toward commercial loggers left the Forest Service in the middle once again, a role that rangers had long experienced.

With budgets nearly doubled after numerous catastrophic fires in the West in the late 1990s, the Forest Service set out on a decades-long plan to manage forests by simulating natural conditions. Every year it used an arsenal of methods to clean a small, but growing, proportion of its stewardship, through limited clear-cutting, extensive thinning, and mechanical cleaning such as piling and chipping. Yet even as it is undoing past mismanagement practices, the Forest Service is enhancing its capability to aggressively fight the especially dangerous "hot" fires that earlier policies spawned. The Forest Service can gauge its political success by keeping the ecological and commercial interests equally dissatisfied with its multiuse policy philosophy, while simultaneously gaining their respect for the integrity of their day-to-day practices.

The competencies necessary for success are readily identified. Technically, the Forest Service is mandated to provide ecological, biological, and horticultural expertise by developing forest management plans that reflect the state of the art and the needs of society. Ethically, it is obligated to ensure compliance with success of those policies by building trust among competing commercial, recreational, and ecological interests and by making prudent decisions, especially when they acknowledge the inadequacy of past decisions. Finally, the agency must be a leader by proposing new policies when old ones have become inadequate, working with Congress and the president to build a coalition to adopt new approaches, and by marshaling resources to clean up thousands of square miles of forest.

Collecting the Trash

Provision of services also includes those that are essential, if mundane, such as water, electricity, and, in this case, trash collection; professional technical, ethical, and leadership skill is vital to ensure health and safety. Such community needs have been furnished by either the private or public sector, depending on local circumstances, and privatization debates have been ongoing for years (Buchanan and Tullock 1962; Niskanen 1971). What delivery model provides the best technical service? How can ethical accountability for cost, dependability, and cleanliness be assured? Who can provide the leadership to supply services and address the needs of those providing them? What represents best practice is the professional edge—technical, ethical, and leadership competencies. The controversy is over criteria about how basic utility functions should be provided: civic necessity (driven by concerns for universal service and public control) or private service (driven by cost factors and customer selection); of course, mixed models are also possible.

Arguments for public provision have generally been:

(a) the efficiency and effectiveness of economies of scale,
(b) the dependability of the government,
(c) the expense of infrastructure development, and
(d) the relatively benign nature of a public monopoly in comparison to the private monopoly that often replaces it.

On the side of providing such services through the private sector, it is commonly claimed that:

(a) the principle of limited government requires the intervention of government to be as restricted as possible,
(b) entrepreneurialism is more efficient and cost conscious by its nature, and
(c) big government tends to usurp too many resources from the economy. See Van Wart, Rahm, and Sanders 2000 for an expansion of the arguments; consult Boyne 1998 for a discussion of why the data on both sides are so confounding.

The preferred approach for basic utilities has vacillated over time, unlike, for example, public safety (governmental role) and human services (nonprofit).

Garbage collection and landfill services provide a good case of changing preferences. Through the 1960s, most cities provided collection services. Such services tended to be characterized by high quality in pickup frequency, cost, and prevention of loose debris. However, some private providers were meeting those standards by the 1970s and 1980s, and many local jurisdictions looked for new models. For example, the city of Phoenix let bids on a number of its collection districts, and city workers lost a number of the districts initially, forcing them to work both harder and smarter. Eventually they won all the districts back through efficiency and aggressive cost savings such as two-person trucks and side-load automatic lifts. Another model popular for small towns has been complete privatization. Many cities such as Conroe, Texas, and Roxboro, North Carolina, have gotten out of the business in the past few years ("Landfill Closure Necessitates Privatized Waste Collection" 1998; "Town Expands Trash Collection Contract" 2002). As it turns out, the public is relatively indifferent to who provides utility services as long as the quality remains high, cost low, and corruption at tolerable levels.

Citizens, then, seem comfortable with either sector providing service so long as it is technically proficient (e.g., timely and clean) and ethically fair (e.g., does not raise rates beyond inflation because it is a monopoly). However, people generally expect the government to exercise leadership in deciding what the delivery service will be and how it will be maintained or regulated over time (e.g., as with cable TV, which is often provided by the private sector but monitored by cities).

Many issues need to be considered before privatization is adopted. In the case of garbage and landfill services, how will the company perform after several years? Will it fall prey to inefficiencies and pass those on to the customers? Is some sort of regulation necessary to replace the direct provision of public services? If the service remains publicly funded but privately provided, does the organization have adequate contract management skills (Ernst 1998)? And finally, because competition may be the best means of ensuring long-term efficiency (Holzer 1998), how can it be institutionalized?

Case Summary

The preceding vignettes provide insight into how difficult it is to be a public service professional; what is easy is seldom excellent. First, in technical terms, cyberwarriors must ensure that the country can defend against "glaring vulnerabilities in our critical information infrastructures" before launching a preemptive strike (Appel 2003). Likewise, forest rangers must undo years of flawed policies that have left natural resources unnecessarily vulnerable to catastrophe. And municipal utility officials have to decide if government or private vendors can provide the most cost-effective service.

Second, ethical demands on professionals are substantial. Public health and safety decisions are integral to national defense, fire management, and garbage collection. Indeed, public service professionals, by definition, handle critical social responsibilities to ensure quality of life. Yet these crucial decisions are often made with complex, competing interests that are difficult to resolve with anything more than an attempt at equity and compassion.

Third, an important dimension of leadership is the creation of a new vision. Foreseeing a new type of warfare in cyberspace is one example. The Forest Service is another illustration of the need for policy change. And trash removal has been revolutionized by leadership that sought technological innovations and demanded new work practices. The public service of tomorrow, in short, must be led by consummate professionals steeped in technical and ethical competencies. The need for such leaders is demonstrated by the Enron Era, itself an outgrowth of the Savings and Loan wildfire discussed in the preceding chapter.

The Enron Era: Perils and Prospects

If the S&L tragedy of the late 1980s and early 1990s is a parable of deregulation, then the perdition of the Enron Era a mere ten years later also symbolizes corporate fraud enabled by government. Like the S&L fiasco, the new scandal, involving numerous companies, revealed the nexus between the public and private sectors. More than fifty senior officials from the Enron Corporation (www.Enron.com) alone, for example, hold important posts in the current administration and many members of Congress received campaign contributions from the energy giant. Politicians, on behalf of their corporate benefactors, have deregulated markets, limited liability, minimized reporting requirements, underfunded oversight agencies, and intervened to protect businesses from scrutiny. The injustice of the Enron Era is that firms are rewarded for lobbying prowess rather than for producing honest goods and services (Mallaby 2002; for an overview of pertinent issues as of 2002, consult www.pbs.org/wgbh/pages/frontline/shows/regulation/).

What follows below is a brief look at the past and future of the scandal, and how:

- the two major scandals compare,
- controls failed,
- the Enron bankruptcy occurred,
- government responded,
- leaders did little to protect the public, and
- the crisis may—or may not—be resolved.

The ultimate miscarriage of the Era, what *Fortune* magazine characterized as "a system failure"(Nocera 2002) is that few of the thousands of professionals involved properly exercised their technical, ethical, and leadership responsibilities.

The Past

This latest scourge of white-collar malfeasance might seem like more of the same. Enron's accountant, Arthur Andersen, for instance, was involved in the S&L crisis and other scandals throughout the 1990s; Kelly 2002) but the current calamity undermines the foundation of free enterprise. Representing technical, ethical, and leadership bankruptcy, Enron was both a creator and product of a system characterized by unregulated profiteering, creative

accounting, offshore tax havens, money laundering, price goug-
ing, permissive boards of directors, executive self-dealing, and
complicit elected officials. The demise of dot-coms in 2000 had
raised questions about artificially inflated profits, but the spec-
tacular 2001 collapse of Enron, which called itself "the World's
Greatest Company," sparked a series of ongoing corporate implo-
sions. Over 1,000 blue chip companies have had to restate their
earnings, and serious harm has been inflicted on shareholders,
employees, and the citizenry. As of fall 2002, the scandals had led
to a collective loss of some $700 billion in shareholder value
(Huffington 2003). The damage to the economic health and well-
being of the nation, brought about by the worst decline in the markets since the Great Depression, is at least as great as that wrought
by other terrorists.

Both internal and external controls, rife with conflicts of interest, failed. The system to protect the public interest was compromised by:

- company boards, whose members provide oversight;
- auditors, who certify the accuracy of books;
- outside law firms, who supply corporate clients with legal
  opinions;
- professional associations, who formulate standards of practice;
- credit rating analysts, who gauge the financial health of businesses;
- brokerage firm analysts, who furnish investment advice;
- mutual fund and pension managers, who do independent
  analyses of businesses they invest in; and
- Securities and Exchange Commission (SEC) regulators, who
  review financial statements.

Enron was founded in 1986, a time when energy production
was a publicly sanctioned monopoly. That changed when the federal government deregulated natural gas and electricity production a few years later, and Enron—honored by *Fortune* magazine
as "America's most innovative company"—emerged as the sev-

enth largest corporation in the nation and the dominant force in trading energy contracts. The fundamental problem, however, was a defective business plan: Large profits from energy trading could not be gained honestly. Indeed, on several occasions the board of directors waived the company's code of ethics, which prohibited some of the problems that arose. Furthermore, in 1997 Enron obtained an SEC exemption from a law barring debts from being shifted off the books and executives from investing in partnerships affiliated with the company.

Through a variety of complex accounting maneuvers involving thousands of shell partnerships, the company inflated profits and lowered debt, misleading unsuspecting investors and the general public about its financial condition. The Private Securities Litigation Reform Act of 1995 made much of this not only possible, but likely (Labaton 2002c). The accounting industry—which had to pay over $1 billion in damages from the S&L crisis—ensured that the law shielded auditors from liability for false reporting and made it difficult for shareholders to bring suit.

Once exposed, it was clear that the Enron scandal—which for a short time was the largest financial fraud in corporate history—had all the features of a Shakespearean drama including ambition, avarice, arrogance, anguish, and death (one executive, as he prepared to testify, allegedly committed suicide). Company stock dropped from nearly $90 a share to less than $1, thousands of employees lost their jobs and retirement savings, and executives reaped millions by selling stock before the corporation's demise. The calamity shook markets, as investors feared that other companies engaged in fraudulent accounting practices, a fear realized as a long, and growing, list of them are under scrutiny: Adelphia Communications Corporation, AOL-Time Warner, Bristol-Myers-Squibb, Duke Energy, Dynegy, Merck and Company, Centennial Technologies, Edison Schools, Global Crossing Ltd., Fannie Mae, Halliburton, HealthSouth, Tenent Healthcare Corporation, Homestore, ImClone Systems Inc., Kmart, Lucent Technologies, Merrill-Lynch, Qwest International Communications, General Electric Corporation, Martha Stewart Living, OmniMedia, Phar-

Mor, Rite Aid, Sunbeam, Salomon Smith Barney, Sprint, Waste Management, WorldCom, Xerox, Tyco International Limited, UnumProvident—and leading banks (such as J.P. Morgan, Chase, Citigroup) that facilitated the duplicitous transactions. Greed and criminality would later spread to the nation's $7 trillion mutual fund industry. Indeed, the usual way the mass media labels a scandal (by applying the suffix "-gate" to the problem) does not apply because so many organizations are involved (for running tallies, see www.citizenworks.org and www.thecorporatelibrary.com).

In 2002, Congress passed the Sarbanes-Oxley bill (or the Public Company Accounting Reform and Investor Protection Act) imposing new corporate governance standards and reporting requirements on publicly traded companies, their accountants, and their attorneys. See Bronner 2003 on the need for a similar law covering governmental entities. These include issues of executive liability, compensation, conflicts of interest, and financial disclosure. Critics charge, however, that many key concerns were not addressed: (a) restoring a Depression-era law holding investment bankers, lawyers, and auditors liable for fraud, (b) providing for effective rules to prohibit accounting firms from selling consulting services to the same companies they audit, (c) closing the revolving door between auditors and clients, (d) establishing a new regulatory board over accounting firms, and (e) dealing with energy regulation and campaign finance reform (Labaton 2002c; www.enronwatchdog.org). Despite, or perhaps because of, the new law, there has been a record number of shareholder resolutions introduced at annual meetings seeking to safeguard investments (Deutsch 2003).

Critical to any change is effective enforcement that will require political will to supply more resources than agencies have or are likely to receive. In 1980, for instance, the SEC checked all company filings; in 2002, it examined only 8 percent of them as the Commission has had to rely on industry self-regulation ("Watching the Watchers" 2002). Thus, the agency, charged to review 17,000 companies, oversee mutual funds, vet brokerage firms, ensure proper operation of exchanges, and guard against market manipulation and accounting misconduct, does not have sufficient staff to "even read annual reports" (Nocera 2002). Too, employee turnover is double that of the rest of government. "The cost of not funding the SEC," writes *Fortune* reporter Clifton Leaf, "is more disasters like Enron" (Nocera 2002).

As in the S&L fiasco, few leaders have emerged during the crisis to protect citizens because so many played an integral role in the scandal itself. Paralleling the earlier debacle, politicians of both parties were so compromised by contributions from firms urging deregulation, that rules were changed providing opportunities for corruption. Because they helped create the problem, there were not many professionals ready to put the national interest ahead of greed, ideology, or campaign funds. However, two officials— Arthur Levitt and Eliot Spitzer—should be noted. Levitt, SEC chairman during the 1990s, attacked conflicts of interest, struggled to improve accounting practices, and vigorously opposed the 1995 law. But ultimately he was thwarted because it became clear that the Commission's appropriations would be jeopardized if he did not withdraw his objections.

New York Attorney General Eliot Spitzer—in the face of considerable political opposition—aggressively investigated Wall Street brokerage houses in what would be the largest case of consumer fraud ever. This was in response to revelations that investors lost millions after being advised to buy stock in Enron (and many other firms) that analysts privately derided as a "POS" (piece of sh*t) to lure companies to become their investment banking clients. In 2003, ten of the country's top brokerages agreed to pay nearly $1.5 billion to resolve the charges. Critics of the settlement (e.g., Huffington 2003) argued that it did not require any admission of guilt or prison sentences, and that the fines, which are tax deductible and/or covered by insurance, are a small fraction of what companies received and investors lost. Spitzer maintains that the entire financial reporting system "will be much stronger . . . and there will be . . . a greater degree of integrity. We need to see how Wall Street implements this deal" (Schlosser 2003). There was speculation that Spitzer may have concluded that attacking the most powerful people in the nation might not be prudent for someone interested in higher office.

The Future

Court settlements, such as the one above, are preferred for many reasons: the costs to both the defense and prosecution, the embarrassment to the accused of a public trial, understaffed prosecutor offices lacking background to pursue complex securities cases, difficulty in proving wrongdoing beyond reasonable doubt, and an overall concern about the socioeconomic consequences of guilty verdicts against major corporations. Indeed, high profile, "rotten apple" prosecutions, their settlements, and rare guilty verdicts actually may blunt more effective, systemic change.

One knowledgeable attorney pointed out that the dynamic is one of swift justice, slow reform: "If I were heading the lobbying coalition against (reform), I'd be happy about the human sacrifices as the best way to placate these gods. That's the way it works" (quoted in Labaton 2002a). Thus, the conviction of Enron's accounting firm in 2002 may serve as a warning to auditors tempted to keep clients satisfied, but it may not lead to genuine change (Hilzenrath 2002). Arthur Levitt said, "It is appalling that the clout of the accounting industry may yet keep Congress from adopting meaningful laws" (Labaton 2002b). Among prominent cases, forty-seven executives at seven corporations have been indicted and twenty have pleaded guilty; the investigations will take years to complete ("Corporate Scandals" 2003).

The solutions to the current crisis are as obvious as they are likely to be ignored insofar as past initiatives to improve corporate activities have been thwarted by sham reforms and political donations. As Barbara Roper, director of investor protection at the Consumer Federation of America, opined, "The way this may play out is that you will see a wad of bills proposed. The ones that may have some traction are the ones that don't do much, but allow members (of Congress) to say they did something" (Labaton 2002b).

Using the competency triangle, it is clear that from a technical perspective accounting rules and disclosure requirements need substantive improvement, as Arthur Andersen's practices were no worse than those of other accounting houses (Apostolou and Thibadoux 2003). Ethically, organizations should enhance their infrastructures (chapter 3), be placed under a court-appointed surveillance supervisor, and be required to advertise their wrongdoing. And disgraced executives should be required to return illicit monies, make restitution, and serve time in prison. Finally, leaders must address the root causes of the problem—business deregulation, Wall Street demands for short-term financial results, public oversight eviscerated by political pressure, private campaign financing, and overall failure of professionals to protect the populace.

Indeed, the ease with which organized crime infiltrated unscrupulous brokerage firms (Weiss 2003) illustrates how readily technical expertise, ethical integrity, and competent leadership can be subverted. The crisis made clear that professional norms may be necessary but are insufficient as opportunism, expediency, and easy money can readily trump fiduciary responsibilities. As Edmund Burke famously observed, "All that is necessary for evil to triumph is for good men to do nothing." Unless progress occurs in these areas, more execrable enterprises like Enron can be expected.

"Ultimately capitalism will almost certainly survive this onslaught from the capitalists—if only because survival is the most profitable outcome for all concerned" (Eichenwald 2002). Yet if such a built-in chastening corrective operates, it does so only after substantial damage occurs; by the time the market recognizes fraud, financial—and social—capital is gone. A more constructive, preventive approach includes:

- establishment of an official Commission on White-Collar Crime, headed by someone like Arthur Levitt, to develop a comprehensive strategy to address the problem (Barbash 2002);

- appointment of a federal independent Special Counsel, such as Elliot Spitzer, to investigate wrongdoing;
- redefinition of the terms of state charters that permit existence of public corporations (Kelly 2001; www.poclad.org);
- a high profile "war on fraud," led by the nation's first president who holds an MBA, to restore citizen trust;
- reconstituting of business schools, "silent partners" in corporate sleaze, in order to produce better graduates; and
- rediscovery of the *raison d'être* of professionalism—technical, ethical, and leadership competence.

Until such a time, what makes pervasive corporate crime not just a business scandal but also a political one is that there is no consistent countervailing power to corporate influence on the policy-making process of the nation. "One of the most important duties of government," wrote William Jennings Bryant more than 100 years ago, "is to put rings in the noses of hogs."

Conclusion

The public service—with its historic past, demanding present, and challenging future—offers both hope and despair for the future. But what is to come is not an inevitable product of large-scale demographic, economic, or political trends. Instead, it will be determined by the culmination of day-to-day decisions in public agencies, not-for-profit organizations, and private contractors. If those decisions are to serve the interests of the agency's varied publics, then they ought to be made in ways that reflect high degrees of responsiveness, accountability, and professionalism. Such actions, even when incorrect, are more likely to serve society's ideals than those made without transparency and respect for the commonweal.

While managers in today's multisectored public service promote these standards, not all do as this book has shown. Professionals need to be responsible to themselves, their agencies, and the populace. The discussion in these pages has sought to prepare current and prospective officials for this challenge by fostering technical expertise, ethical integrity, and leadership ability. The goal was to encourage reflection on the nature of professionalism as the new century unfolds. There is no time like the present to set higher standards; no one ever regretted doing his best. If readers finish this book with a renewed desire to hone their professional edge, then that objective will have been achieved.

References

Alabama Department of Rehabilitation Services, Customer Support System. 2001. Montgomery, AL: Alabama Department of Rehabilitation Services.

American Society for Public Administration. 2000. *Performance Measurement: Concepts and Techniques.* Washington, DC: ASPA.

Ammons, D. 2002. *Tools for Decision Making: A Practical Guide for Local Government.* Washington, DC: CQ Press.

Anderson, A. 1996. *Ethics and Fundraising.* Bloomington: Indiana University Press.

Andrisani, P., S. Hakim, and E. Leeds. 2000. *Making Government Work.* New York: Rowman & Littlefield.

Anon. 2002. "An Aesthetic Theory of Conflict in Administrative Ethics." Unpublished manuscript.

Apostolou, B., and G. Thibadoux. 2003. "Why Integrity Matters: Accounting for the Accountants." *Public Integrity* 5, no. 3: 223–38.

Appel, E. 2003. "Information Security Must Catch Up with Cybercriminals." *Federal Times*, March 10: 21.

Associated Press. 2003. "Charity Pulls Money from Some Branches of Salvation Army: United Way Says Offices Didn't Meet Agency's Standards." *Lansing State Journal.* Available at: www.lsj.com/news/local/030227_charity_2b.html.

Aulisio, M., R. Arnold, and S. Youngner. 2000. "Health Care Ethics Consultation: Nature, Goals, and Competencies." *Annals of Internal Medicine* 133, no. 1: 59–69.

Bailey, S. 1965. "Relationship Between Ethics and Public Service." In *Public Administration and Democracy: Essays in Honor of Paul Appleby*, ed. R. Martin, 282–98. Syracuse, NY: Syracuse University Press.

Barbash, F. 2002. "It's Time to Punish Corporate Sinners." *Washington Post National Weekly Edition*, July 15–21: 21.

Bass, B. 1985. *Leadership and Performance Beyond Expectations.* New York: Free Press.

———. 1990. *Bass & Stogdill's Handbook of Leadership.* New York: Free Press.

Belker, L. 1997. *The First-Time Manager.* New York: AMACOM.

Berkowitz, B. 2003. *The New Face of War: How War Will Be Fought in the 21st Century.* New York: Free Press.

Berman, E. 1998. *Productivity Improvement in Public and Nonprofit Organizations.* Thousand Oaks, CA: Sage.

Berman, E., and J. West, 1998. "Productivity Enhancement Efforts in Public and Nonprofit Organizations." *Public Productivity & Management Review* 22, no. 2: 207–19.

Berman, E., J. Bowman, J. West, and M. Van Wart. 2001. *Human Resource Management in Public Service*. Thousand Oaks, CA: Sage.

Blair, B. 2002. "The Ultimate Management Challenge." *Federal Times*, November 25: 1, 6.

Bloom, A. 1988. *The Closing of the American Mind: How Higher Education Has Failed Democracy and Impoverished the Souls of Today's Students*. New York: Simon and Schuster.

Bok, D. 1986. *Higher Learning*. Cambridge, MA: Harvard University Press.

Bolman, L., and T. Deal. 1991. *Reframing Organizations*. San Francisco: Jossey-Bass.

Bowman, J. 1998. *"The Lost World* of Public Administration Education: Rediscovering the Meaning of Professionalism." *Journal of Public Affairs Education* 4, no. 1: 27–31.

———. 2000. "From Codes of Conduct to Codes of Ethics." In *Handbook of Administrative Ethics*, ed. T. Cooper, 335–54. New York: Dekker.

———. 2002. "A Naked Formula to Corrupt the Public Service." *WorkingUSA* 51 (Fall): 90–102.

———. 2003. "Virtue Ethics." *Encyclopedia of Public Administration and Public Policy*, ed. J. Rabin, 1259–63. New York: Dekker.

Bowman, J., and R. Williams. 1997. "Ethics in Government: From a Winter of Despair to a Spring of Hope." *Public Administration Review* 57: 517–26.

Boyne, G. 1998. "Bureaucratic Theory Meets Reality: Public Choice and Service Contracting in U.S. Local Government." *Public Administration Review* 58, no. 6: 474–84.

Bronner, K. 2003. "Does Government Need a Sarbanes-Oxley Type Reform Act?" *PA Times* (April): 6–7.

Brousseau, P. 1998. "Ethical Dilemmas: Right vs. Right." In *The Ethics Edge*, ed. E. Berman, J. West, and S. Bonczek, 35–46. Washington, DC: International City/County Management Association.

Brown, S. 1987. *Thirteen Fatal Errors Managers Make and How You Can Avoid Them*. New York: Berkley Publishing Group.

Bruce, W. 1996. "Codes of Ethics and Codes of Conduct: Perceived Contribution to the Practice of Ethics in Local Government." *Public Integrity Annual*: 23–30.

Bryson, J. 1995. *Strategic Planning for Public and Nonprofit Organizations: A Guide to Strengthening and Sustaining Organizational Achievement*. San Francisco: Jossey-Bass.

Brzezinksi, M. 2003. "The Unmanned Army." *New York Times Sunday Magazine*, April 20: 38–41, 80.

Buchanan, J., and G. Tullock. 1962. *The Calculus of Consent*. Ann Arbor: University of Michigan Press.

Carney, G. 1998. "Working Paper: Conflict of Interest: Legislators, Ministers, and Public Officials." Available at: www.transparency.org/working_papers/carney/4–conclusions.html (accessed June 4, 2003).

Carroll, J. 2002. "A New Management Agenda for the Federal Government?" *PA Times* (January): 9.

Cohen, S., and W. Eimicke. 2002. *The Effective Public Manager.* San Francisco: Jossey-Bass.

Cohen, S., W. Eimicke, and J. Horan. 2002. "Catastrophe and the Public Service: A Case Study of the Government Response to the Destruction of the World Trade Center." *Public Administration Review* 62 (special issue): 24–32.

Columbia Accident Investigation Board. 2003. *Report.* Washington, DC: Government Printing Office.

Condrey, S., and R. Maranto. 2001. *Radical Reform of the Civil Service.* Lanham, MD: Lexington Books.

Conlow, R., E. Cohen, J. Zayszly, and R. Mapson. 2001. *Excellence in Supervision: Essential Skills for the New Supervisor.* Menlo Park, CA: Crisp Publications.

Cooper, T., and D. Yoder 2002. "Public Management Ethics Standards in a Transnational World." *Public Integrity* 2, no. 4: 332–52.

Coplin, W., and C. Dwyer. 2000. *Does Your Government Measure Up?* Syracuse, NY: Syracuse University Press.

"Corporate Scandals: A User's Guide." 2003. *New York Times*, Week in Review, May 21: 2.

Council for Excellence in Government. 1998. *Ethical Principles for Public Servants.* Washington, DC: Brookings Institution.

Davidson, D. 2002. "Plugging the Brain Drain." *Federal Times*, November 18: 1, 11.

Deep, S., and L. Sussman. 1992. *What to Say to Get What You Want: Strong Words for Forty-Four Challenging Types of Bosses, Employees, Coworkers and Customers.* New York: Addison-Wesley.

de Leon, P. 1993. *Thinking About Political Corruption.* Armonk, NY: M.E. Sharpe.

Denhardt, R., and J. Denhardt. 2001. "Selfless Public Servants Stand Apart in Heroic Response." *Public Administration Times*, September 24: 19.

———. 2003. *The New Public Service: Serving, Not Steering.* Armonk, NY: M.E. Sharpe.

DelPo, A., and L. Guerin. 2003. *Dealing with Problem Employees.* 2d ed. Berkeley, CA: Nolo Press.

DePree, M. 1989. *Leadership Is an Art.* New York: Doubleday.

Deutsch, C. 2003. "Revolt of the Shareholders." *New York Times*, February 23, BU: 1, 12.

DiConti, V. 1998. "Resolution Trust Corporation." In *A Historical Guide to the U.S. Government*, ed. G. Kurian, 510–11. New York: Oxford University Press.

Di Nino, C. 1996. *How to Survive Bad Bosses.* Long Island City, NY: Bright Books.

DiNome, J., S. Yaklin, and D. Rosenbloom. 1999. "Employee Rights: Avoiding Legal Liability." In *Human Resource Management in Local Government: An Essential Guide*, ed. S. Freyss, 93–132. Washington, DC: International City/County Management Association.

Dionne, E. 2001. "Political Hacks v. Bureaucrats." *Brookings Review* 19, no. 2: 8–11.

Dubnick, M. 1998. "Forest Service." In *An Historical Guide to the U.S. Government*, ed. G.T. Kurian, 255–60. New York: Oxford University Press.

Eichenwald, K. 2002. "Could Capitalists Actually Bring Down Capitalism?" *New York Times*, July 30: 1, 5.

Emerson, J. 2003. "Lonely at the Top? Be a Mentor." *Federal Times*, August 4: 16.

Ernst, J. 1998. "Privatization," In *The International Encyclopedia of Public Policy and Administration*, ed. J. M. Shafritz, 1741–45. Boulder, CO: Westview Press.

Fairholm, G. 1991. *Values Leadership: Toward a New Philosophy of Leadership*. New York: Praeger.

Fiedler, F., M. Chemers, and L. Mahar. 1976. *Improving Leadership Effectiveness: The Leader Match Concept*. New York: Wiley.

Flaherty, M., S. Goo, D. Hilzenrath, and J. Grimaldi. 2003. "A Troubled History: *Columbia* Experienced Myriad Problems Before Its Doomed Flight." *Washington Post National Weekly Edition*, March 23–29: 8–9.

Frame, D. 2002. *The New Project Management: Tools for an Age of Rapid Change, Corporate Reengineering, and Other Business Realities*. 2d ed. New York: Wiley.

Frederickson, H.G. 2003. "Clothed in the Public Interest." *PA Times* (April): 11.

———. 2002. "Arthur Andersen, Where Art Thou?" *Public Administration Times* (October): 9.

French, J., and B. Raven. 1959. "The Bases of Social Power." In *Studies of Social Power*, ed. D. Cartwright, 150–67. Ann Arbor, MI: Institute for Social Research.

Friedman, T. 2002. "In Oversight We Trust." *New York Times*, July 28: 13. Available at: www.doi.gov/hrm/pmanager/gm2d.html.

Gellerman, S. 1986. "Why 'Good' Managers Make Bad Ethical Choices." *Harvard Business Review* 64 (July–August): 85–90.

Gilman, S. 1999. "Effective Management of Ethical Systems: Some New Frontiers." In *Fighting Corruption*, ed. V. Mavaso and D. Balia, 95–114. Pretoria: University of South Africa Press.

Graham, B. 2003. "In the New Warfare, It's Computer vs. Computer." *Washington Post National Weekly Edition* (February 17–23): 29–30.

Gulick, L., and L. Urwick. 1937. *Papers on the Science of Administration*. New York: Institute of Public Administration.

Hersey, P., and K. Blanchard. 1969. "The Life Cycle Theory of Leadership." *Training and Development Journal* 23: 26–34.

Hilzenrath, D. 2002. "Postmortem for a Giant." *Washington Post National Weekly Edition* (June 24–30): 6.

Holdstein, W. 2002. "An Insider's Advice on Corporate Ethics." *New York Times*, November 24, BU: 5.

Holzer, M. 1998. "Productivity." In *The Encyclopedia of Public Policy and Administration*, ed. J. M. Shafritz, 1750–55. Boulder, CO: Westview Press.

Holzer, M., and K. Callahan. 1998. *Government at Work: Best Practices and Model Programs*. Thousand Oaks, CA: Sage.

Huffington, A. 2003. *Pigs at the Trough: How Corporate Greed and Political Corruption Are Undermining America*. New York: Crown.

Hutchins, G. 1997. "The Certified Quality Manager." *Quality Digest* (February): 33–38.

Jalandoni, M., L. Lampkin, T. Pollak, and M. Weitzman, eds. 2002. *The New Nonprofit Almanac and Desk Reference*. San Francisco: Jossey-Bass.

Jurkiewicz, C., and K. Nichols. 2002. "Ethics Education in the MPA Curriculum: What Difference Does It Make?" *Journal of Public Affairs Education* 8, no. 2: 103–14.

Katz, R. 1955. "The Skills of an Effective Administrator." *Harvard Business Review* 55: 33–42.

Katzenbach, J., and Smith, D. 1993. *The Wisdom of Teams: Creating the High Performance Organization.* Boston: Harvard Business School Press.

Kaufman, H. 1960. *The Forest Ranger.* Baltimore: Johns Hopkins University Press.

Kaufman, T. 2003. "What Feds Like and Don't Like." *Federal Times,* March 31: 1, 6.

Kaye, J., and M. Allison. 1997. *Strategic Planning for Nonprofit Organizations: A Practical Guide and Workbook.* New York: John Wiley, and Support Center for Nonprofit Management.

Keene, W. 2003. "A Sore that Needs Healing." *Federal Times,* August 12: 15.

Kelly, J. 2002. "Andersen Has Been There Before." *Tallahassee Democrat,* January 18: 1, 6E.

Kelly, M. 2001. *The Divine Right of Capital.* San Francisco: Berrett-Koehler.

Kidder, R. 1994. *Shared Values for a Troubled World: Conversations with Men and Women of Conscience.* San Francisco: Jossey-Bass.

Kettl, D. 2000. *The Global Public Management Revolution.* Washington, DC: Brookings Institution.

———. 2002a. "Managing Indirect Government." In *The Tools of Government: A Guide to the New Governance,* ed. L. Salamon, 490–510. New York: Oxford University Press.

———. 2002b. *The Transformation of Governance: Public Administration for the Twenty-First Century.* Baltimore: Johns Hopkins University Press.

Kobrak, P. 2002. *Cozy Politics: Political Parties, Campaign Finance, and Compromised Governance.* Boulder, CO: Lynne Rienner.

Kohlberg, L. 1971. "From Is to Ought: How to Commit the Naturalistic Fallacy and Get Away With It in the Study of Moral Development." In *Cognitive Development and Epistemology,* ed. Theodore Mischel, 164–65. New York: Elsevier.

———. 1981. *The Philosophy of Moral Development and the Idea of Justice.* New York: Harper and Row.

Kung, H. 1998. *A Global Ethic for Global Politics and Economics.* New York: Oxford University Press.

Labaton, S. 1998. "The Debacle That Buried Washington: Long After the S&L Crisis, Courts Are Handing Taxpayers a New Bill." *New York Times,* November 22, Section 3: 1, 12.

———. 2002a. "Bush Doctrine: Lock 'Em Up." *New York Times,* January 16, BU: 1, 12.

———. 2002b. "Now Who Exactly Got Us into This Mess?" *New York Times,* February 3, BU: 1, 7.

———. 2002c. "Will Reform with Few Teeth Be Able to Bite?" *New York Times,* September 2, BU: 4.

Labbe, J. 2003. "Private Foundations Are Examined with Jaded Eyes." *Tallahassee Democrat,* May 18: 2E.

"Landfill Closure Necessitates Privatized Waste Collection." 1998. *American City & County* 113, no. 9: 14.

"Leadership Is Needed." 2003. *Federal Times*, April 28: 20.

Lee, C. 2003. "The Workers Are Getting Restless." *Washington Post National Weekly Edition*, March 31–April 6: 34.

Lee, M. 2003. "Noncredit Certificates in Nonprofit Management: An Exploratory Study." Milwaukee: University of Wisconsin-Milwaukee (Department of Governmental Affairs). Unpublished paper.

Leicht, K., and M. Fennell. 2001. *Professional Work: A Sociological Approach.* Malden, MA: Blackwell.

Lewis, C. 1998. "Strategies and Tactics for Managerial Decision Making." In *The Ethics Edge*, ed. E. Berman, J. West, and S. Bonczek, 123–29. Washington, DC: International City/County Management Association.

———. 2002. *The Enron Collapse: A Financial Scandal Rooted in Politics.* Washington, DC: Center for Public Integrity.

Light, P. 1997. *The Tides of Reform.* Washington, DC: Brookings Institution.

———. 1999. *The New Public Service.* Washington, DC: Brookings Institution.

Liles, R. 2003. "United Way Still a Vital Part of Our Community." *Lansing State Journal.* Available at: www.lsj.com/opinions/letters/030316_lilesptv_ (un.html).

Linden, R. 1995. *Seamless Government: A Practical Guide to Re-engineering in the Public Sector.* San Francisco: Jossey-Bass.

Mackenzie, G., and J. Labiner. 2002. "Opportunity Lost: The Rise and Fall of Confidence." In *Government after September 11.* Washington, DC: Brookings Institution. www.brook.edu/dybdocroot/gs/cps/opportunityfinal.pdf (accessed on September 24, 2002).

Mallaby, S. 2002. "A Worm at the Core of Capitalism." *Washington Post National Weekly Edition*, June 17–23: 26.

Martin, T. 2003. "Fraud, Forgery on the Rise: Expert Says Firms Now More Likely to Report Crimes." *Lansing State Journal.* Available at: www.lsj.com/news/local/030227_fraud_1a-5a.html.

Matthews, J. 2003. *The Lawsuit Survival Guide: A Client's Companion to Litigation.* Berkeley, CA: Nolo Press.

McClelland, D. 1985. *Human Motivation.* Glenview, IL: Scott, Foresman.

McFadden, R. 2003. "A Revolutionary Program Troubled from the Start." *New York Times*, February 2: 1, 18.

Mead, M. 2001. *New Lives for Old: Cultural Transformation—Manus.* New York: Harper-Collins.

Melot, D. 2003a. "Charity's 'Myth' Stifles Inquiries: United Way Isn't the Only Way to Foster Giving." *Lansing State Journal.* Available at: www.lsj.com/columnists/melot/030114_melot_(top).html.

———. 2003b. "United Way: Reforms Look Promising, but Tests of Trust Remain." *Lansing State Journal.* Available at: www.lsj.com/opinions/editorials/030525eds1_(united_way).html.

Menzel, D. 1997. "Teaching Ethics and Values in Public Administration: Are We Making a Difference?" *Public Administration Review* 57: 224–30.

Menzel, D. with C. Carson. 1997. "Empirical Research on Public Administration Ethics: A Review and Assessment." *Public Integrity* 1, no. 3: 239–64.

Mintz, J. 2003. "Ridge's Rise to Homeland Security." *Washington Post National Weekly Edition*, March 10–16: 29.

Morin, R., and C. Deane. 2002. "From Crisis, Growth and Change." *Washington Post Weekly*, September 16–22: 34.

Mosher, F. 1982. *Democracy and the Public Service*. New York: Oxford University Press.

National Academy of Public Administration. 2003. *The 21st Century Manager: A Study of Changing Roles and Competencies*. Washington, DC: Academy.

National Commission on the Public Service. 2003. *Urgent Business for America: Revitalizing the Federal Government for the 21st Century*. Washington, DC: Brookings Institution.

National Fire Plan Implementation. 2001. Subcommittee on Forests and Forest Health of the Committee on Resources, U.S. House of Representatives, March 8, Serial No. 107-3 (Document ID f: 70955.wais).

Niskanen, W. 1971. *Bureaucracy and Representative Government*. Chicago: Aldine-Altherton.

Nocera, J. 2002. System Failure: "Corporate America Has Lost Its Way." *Fortune*, June 9. Available at: www.fortune.com.

Northouse, P. 2003. *Leadership: Theory and Practice*. 3d ed. Thousand Oaks, CA: Sage.

O'Neill, R., and Christopher, G. 2002. "Wildfire Protection: A Lesson in Management." *Federal Times*, October 7: 28.

Osborne, D., and P. Plastrik. 1998. *Banishing Bureaucracy: The Five Strategies for Reinventing Government*. New York: Penguin Putnam.

Ottaway, D., and J. Stephens. 2003. "Big Green: The Nature Conservancy Builds Its Assets with Some Surprising Corporate Partners." *Washington Post National Weekly Edition*, May 12–18: 6–7.

Paine, L. 1994. "Managing for Organizational Integrity." *Harvard Business Review* 72, no. 2 (March/April): 106–17.

Pfiffner, J., and D. Brook. 2000. *The Future of Merit: Twenty Years After the Civil Service Reform Act*. Baltimore: Johns Hopkins University Press.

Rainey, H. 1997. "The 'How Much Is Due Process' Debate." In *Handbook of Public Law and Administration*, ed. P. Cooper, 237–53. New York: Marcel Dekker.

Rest, J., and D. Narvez. 1994. *Moral Development in the Professions*. Hillsdale, NJ: Erlbaum.

Reuters. 1996. *Burn Forests to Save Them, Says U.S. Forest Service*." July 30, record number 0D6FE92370B8ACA.

Reynaert, M. 2002. "Statement about Embezzlement by Robert Berning, President, Capital Area United Way" (12–27–02). *Capital Area United Way*. Available at: www.capitalareaunitedway.org/media/122702.htm.

Riccucci, N. 1995. *Unsung Heroes: Federal Execucrats Making a Difference*. Washington, DC: Georgetown University Press.

Rosenbloom, D., and M. Bailey. 2003. "What Every Public Personnel Manager

Should Know About the Constitution." In *Public Personnel Administration*, ed. S. Hays and R. Kerney, 29–45. Upper Saddle River, NJ: Prentice-Hall.

Salamon, L. 2002. "The New Governance and the Tools of Public Action: An Introduction." In *The Tools of Government: A Guide to the New Governance*, ed. Salamon, 1–47. New York: Oxford University Press.

Schlosser, J. 2003. "Spitzer Speaks." *Fortune*, May 27. Available at: www.fortune.com

Shalala, D. 1998. "Are Large Public Organizations Manageable"? *Public Administration Review* 58, no. 4: 284–89.

Sherwood, F. 2000. "Research Needs on the Public Service." In *Public Service: Callings, Commitments, and Contributions*, ed. M. Holzer, 356–70. Boulder, CO: Westview Press.

Snell, R. 1993. *Developing Skills for Ethical Management*. London: Chapman and Hill.

Stogdill, R. 1948. "Personal Factors Associated with Leadership: A Survey of the Literature." *Journal of Psychology* 25: 35–71.

Svara, J. 1997. "The Ethical Triangle." *Public Integrity Annual* 2: 33–41.

Terry, L. 1995. *Leadership of Public Bureaucracies: The Administrator as Conservator*. Thousand Oaks, CA: Sage.

Thompson, D. 1998. "Paradoxes of Government Ethics." In *The Ethics Edge*, ed. E. Berman, J. West, and S. Bonczek, 47–60. Washington, DC: International City/County Management Association.

Thompson, F. 2002. "Introduction: Homeland Security: The State and Local Crunch." *Public Administration Review* 62 (special issue): 19–20.

"Town Expands Trash Collection Contract." 2002. *American City & County* 117, no. 1: 15–18.

Trevino, L., G. Weaver, D. Gibson, and B. Toffler. 1999. "Managing Ethical and Legal Compliance: What Works and What Hurts." *California Management Review* 40 (2): 131–51.

United Nations, General Assembly. 1948. United Nations Universal Declaration on Human Rights. Available at: www.un.org/Overview/rights.

Van Wart, M. 1998. *Changing Public Sector Values*. New York: Garland.

Van Wart, M., D. Rahm, and S. Sanders. 2000. "Economic Development and Public Enterprise: The Case of Rural Iowa's Telecommunications Utilities." *Economic Development Quarterly* 14, no. 2: 131–45.

Ventriss, C., and S. Barney. 2003. "The Making of a Whistleblower and the Impact of Ethical Autonomy: James F. Alderson." *Public Integrity* 5, no. 4: 355–68.

Volcker, P. 2003. *The National Commission on Public Service*. Washington, DC: Brookings Institution.

Walters, J. 2002. *Life After Civil Service Reform*. Washington DC: Pricewaterhouse Coopers Human Capital Series. Available at: www.businessofgovernment.org.

Wartick, S., and D. Wood. 1998. *International Business and Society*. Malden, MA: Blackwell.

"Watching the Watchers." 2002. *Washington Post National Weekly Edition*, May 27–June 2: 24.

Wayne, L. 2002. "For-Profit Secret Army." *New York Times*, October 13, BU: 1, 10–11.

Weber, L. 2002. "Uneasy Giving: Questionable Actions Raise Doubts about United Way." *Chicago Tribune*, November 26: 36.

Weiss, G. 2003. *Born to Steal: When the Mafia Hit Wall Street.* New York: Warner Books.

West, J. 2002. "Georgia on the Mind of Radical Civil Service Reformers." *Review of Public Personnel Administration* 22, no. 2: 79–93.

West, J., and E. Berman. 2001. "From Traditional to Virtual HR: Is the Transition Occurring in Local Government?" *Review of Public Personnel Administration* 21, no. 1: 38–64.

White, L., and L. Lam. 2002. "A Proposed Infrastructural Model of the Establishment of Organizational Ethics Systems." *Journal of Business Ethics* 28: 35–42.

Windt, P., P. Appleby, M. Battin, L. Francis, and B. Landesman, eds. 1989. "Ethical Issues in the Professions." Appendix 11, *Selected Codes of Professional Ethics, Model Rules of Professional Conduct*: 555–66. Englewood Cliffs, NJ: Prentice Hall.

Wise, C. 1996. "Understanding Your Liability as a Public Administrator." In *Handbook of Public Administration*, ed. J. Perry, 713–34. San Francisco: Jossey-Bass.

"Work-force Priority." 2001. *Federal Times*, December 31: 18.

Yukl, G. 1998. *Leadership in Organizations.* 4th ed. Englewood Cliffs, NJ: Prentice-Hall.

Zalenik, A. 1977. "Managers and Leaders: Are They Different?" *Harvard Business Review* 55: 67–78.

Ziegler, M. 2003. "Frightening: Government Lacks Leaders to Coordinate IT Security." *Federal Times*, April 14: 1, 8.

About the Authors

James S. Bowman is professor of public administration at the Askew School of Public Administration and Policy, Florida State University. His primary area is human resource management. Noted for his work in ethics and quality management, Dr. Bowman has also done research in environmental administration. He is author of nearly 100 journal articles and book chapters, as well as editor of five anthologies. Bowman co-wrote, with Evan M. Berman, Jonathan P. West, and Montgomery Van Wart, *Human Resource Management: Paradoxes, Processes, and Problems* in 2001. He is editor-in-chief of *Public Integrity*, a journal sponsored by the American Society for Public Administration, the International City/County Management Association, the Council on Governmental Ethics Laws, the Ethics Resource Center, and the Council on State Governments. Bowman also serves on the editorial boards of three other professional journals. A past national Association of Schools of Public Affairs and Administration Fellow, as well as a Kellogg Foundation Fellow, he has experience in the military, in the civil service, and in business.

Jonathan P. West is professor of political science and director of the Graduate Public Administration program at the University of Miami. His research interests include human resource management, productivity, local government, and ethics. He has written six books and nearly seventy-five articles and book chapters. *Quality Management Today: What Local Government Managers Need to Know* (1995) and *The Ethics Edge* (1998) were published as part of the Practical Management Series by the International City/

County Management Association. His co-authored book, titled *American Politics and the Environment*, was released in 2002. Dr. West is managing editor of *Public Integrity* and a member of the editorial board of two other professional journals. He has experience as a management analyst working for the Office of the Surgeon General, Department of the Army. He is a member of the American Political Association, the American Society for Public Administration, the Western Political Science Association, and the Southern Political Science Association.

Evan M. Berman is associate professor in the Department of Public Administration at the University of Central Florida. He is active in the American Society for Public Administration and was the 1998–2000 chair of the Section of Personnel and Labor Relations. He has written more than seventy-five publications in human resource management, productivity, ethics, and local government. Berman has served on the editorial boards of *Public Administration Review* and the *Review of Public Personnel Administration*. His books include *Productivity in Public and Nonprofit Organizations* (1998) and *Public Sector Performance* (1999). Berman has been a policy analyst with the National Science Foundation and works with numerous local jurisdictions on matters of team building, productivity improvement, strategic planning, and citizen participation.

Montgomery Van Wart is associate professor and head of the Department of Public Administration at the University of Central Florida. He co-wrote *The Handbook of Training and Development for the Public Sector* (1994) and wrote *Changing Public Sector Values* (1998). His research on public sector training and development, organization change, ethics, comparative public administration, leadership, and productivity has appeared in major public administration journals.

Index